NEW PORT RICHEY'S HACIENDA HOTEL

A Haven for Silent Screen Stars, Literati & Sports Legends

GARY VITACCO-ROBLES

THE
History
PRESS

Published by The History Press
Charleston, SC
www.historypress.com

With images from the West Pasco Historical Society.

First published 2024

Manufactured in the United States

ISBN 9781467157544

Library of Congress Control Number: 2024937692

Dedicated to

Oscar Vitacco-Robles,
Bob Langford and Ann Rusaw James,
the Battista family,
Thomas Reed Martin,
George Reginald Sims and Marjorie Byington Sims,
James E. Meighan,
Thomas Meighan,
Warren E. Burns,
James H. Becker,
Caroline Serra Henderson,
Michael Bernstein
and Jim Gunderson, the man who saved the Hacienda Hotel.

CONTENTS

CONTENTS

ACKNOWLEDGEMENTS

I owe deep gratitude to many fine individuals who helped me in this endeavor, a passion project for the Hacienda Hotel on New Port Richey's centennial. I wish to thank all the members of the West Pasco Historical Society Museum and Library for their contributions and for allowing the reproduction of valuable images from their archives. I especially thank Bob Langford, Ann Rusaw James, Tomás Monzón, Paul and Suzie Herman, Beva Stevenson and Mario Caruso, who have all become my friends.

I appreciate the following for their participation in interviews: Regan Weiss, Bob Langford, Dr. Chase DeCubellis, Caroline Serra Henderson, Russ Tanner, Dylan Gamez, Rafe Banks, Danny Banks, Charlene "Charlie" Randall, Haley Schalmo, Beth Whitelaw Fregger, Tina Gordon, Sallie Solie and Oscar Vitacco-Robles. I extend special thanks to members of the Battista family who spoke with me during our wonderful reunion at The Hacienda in 2022: Jackie (Battista) Jackson, John Battista, Tina Battista Bartunek and Michele Battista Hulmes. I especially express thanks to Jim Gunderson for our fireside conversations in The Hacienda's lobby. Thanks to my parents, Frank and Gloria Vitacco; my aunt Priscilla Muralo (whose one hundredth birthday was celebrated at The Hacienda); and my brother, Mark Vitacco (who is a frequent guest of the hotel).

In 2022, No Naked Walls Art and Frame Shop was entrusted to restore, print and frame the archived photographs from the West Pasco Historical Society to be displayed at the much-anticipated reopened Hacienda Hotel. Some of the images in this book are the photographs from that project, which helped bring back to life the early days of New Port Richey. Prints are available at the West Pasco Historical Society, with sales contributing to the group's ongoing work. Thanks to Deb Reinhold of No Naked Walls Art and Frame Shop for her assistance.

Thanks to PICRYL public domain archive and Get Archive LLC for permission to reproduce vintage images and to Jim Gunderson and Tim McClain for permission to reproduce contemporary images of the Hacienda Hotel.

Permission to use the cover images was provided by the West Pasco Historical Society, Jim Gunderson, PICRYL public domain archive and Get Archive LLC.

Thanks to the Library of Congress for images of Raymond Hitchcock.

It takes a village.

INTRODUCTION

New Port Richey is experiencing an exciting renaissance. New energy exudes from Main Street and Grand Boulevard, where young people glide on electric scooters and visitors dine al fresco and socialize on rooftop lounges. Baby boomers on golf carts motor along pub crawls. Couples of all ages stroll together around Orange Lake, and children frolic on splash pads in Sims Park.

As the city's centennial approaches in October 2024, the downtown area is revitalized with business, entertainment, pedestrian traffic, social and cultural events and community pride in New Port Richey's heritage and preservation. The historic district feels reborn as the surrounding area experiences rapid growth and alteration.

These are difficult times for old-time residents of Pasco County. Everything seems to be rapidly changing, vanishing and fading. The bucolic pastures and ranches along the State Road 54 corridor are being replaced with dense housing and retail development. On freshly cleared land, elevator shafts pop up, signaling the construction of multistory apartment complexes. Cows and wildlife are replaced by sport utility vehicles. The foliage is lost to cement and asphalt. Joni Mitchell's melancholic lyrics apply: "They paved paradise and put up a parking lot."

But this book is about preservation, conservancy and restoration. It's about the Hacienda Hotel, an iconic New Port Richey landmark that has been lovingly revived and arguably vastly improved since its original grand opening in 1927. This book is also a tribute to a building that has haunted and inspired me since childhood.

Oscar, my spouse, and I joined the Friends of The Hacienda and Historic New Port Richey, an organization devoted to celebrating the unique history and culture of the city. The grassroots group is dedicated to encouraging community pride and involvement through the development of events and projects that honor the city's past while nurturing its future. Through the Friends of The Hacienda and West Pasco Historical Society, we met and befriended Bob and Ann Langford and Tomás Monzón, residents dedicated to the city's past and future who campaigned to save the hotel.

Along with Bob and Ann, Oscar and I attended the boutique hotel's reopening gala in September 2022 and had the honor of being four of the first guests to spend the first night in the building since it closed decades earlier and lay vacant and in decay, seemingly destined for the wrecking ball.

Personally, I had another reason to celebrate that evening. I fell in love with The Hacienda the first time I saw her.

It was May 1973. I was eight years old and on spring break from St. Kevin's Catholic Academy in Queens, New York, with my parents and aunt and uncle. My family had just purchased three lots on the same street in a new subdivision in New Port Richey on which to build three homes: one for us, one for my aunt and uncle and one for my elderly maternal grandmother and her brother.

After signing contracts for construction with Gary Blackwell of Security Builders, we drove downtown, past the golden dome of the Richey Suncoast Theatre, around Orange Lake and into Sims Park.

And there she was on the corner of Main and Bank Streets: the Hacienda Hotel. My heart stood still. It was love at first sight. The marquee sign announced she was currently serving as a venue for performances by the Ink Spots. At the time, I did not realize the role the historic hotel would play in my life.

I was happy to be living in what was called the "gateway to tropical Florida," and I befriended many whose families had lived here for generations. They warmly welcomed me and have remained lifelong friends.

I avidly researched my new hometown with a specific interest in The Hacienda. During the Chasco Fiesta in Sims Park, I purchased a book titled *West Pasco Heritage* from Julie Obenreder, its author. I read the book so many times, I broke its spine. Through Obenreder's research and a book of historic illustrations of the city by Kathleen Strode, I learned the history of New Port Richey and the role of the Hacienda Hotel in its early development.

Decades before my family relocated from Long Island to New Port Richey, there was another generation of residents from Long Island— Great Neck and King's Point—who formed a winter enclave in the city.

They were silent film and stage actors, professional sportsmen and literati whose names my grandmother recognized. Some of them built The Hacienda, and others were its guests. Several of these luminaries coaxed colleagues from Long Island to the hotel to experience the splendor of the tropical climate and invest in property. In the 1970s, there were plenty of old-timers willing to share their memories of these interesting past residents and their glory days with an interested youth.

My family had season tickets to the Richey Suncoast Theatre, and before the shows, we usually had dinner at the Hacienda Hotel. When I entered the hotel's courtyard, the city seemed to fall away. I found myself in the embrace of a beautiful, sheltered environment. Inside, the aroma of the old building insinuated its history—and a bygone era. Incidentally, I still have a scar on my shin from where I fell off the Richey Suncoast Theatre's stage during a rehearsal; my mother volunteered in the box office for many years, and I designed program covers and painted sets.

When I accompanied my parents to their financial transactions at Ellis First National Bank on U.S. 19—before the days of online banking—I observed in the lobby a large painting of the Hacienda Hotel, proudly displayed as the city's crown jewel. My fascination with it never wavered.

During my junior high and high school days, the Hacienda Hotel remained the cultural and social center of the city.

By the time I attended Gulf Comprehensive High School in the early 1980s, I had befriended John Battista, whose parents owned The Hacienda, where he and his siblings worked. John's garage band, Shadowfax, frequently performed on weekends in a corner of the lobby by the telephone booth, complete with strobe light special effects.

The Hacienda photobombed Polaroid snapshots from my youth and seemed to perpetually haunt me. During a Gulf High homecoming parade, as I roared the Buccaneer football team chant atop a crepe paper–bedecked parade float with my classmates, we passed in front of The Hacienda. During another homecoming parade, as I waved to onlookers in an open Corvette as an escort to Deanna Tudor, a beautiful member of the Homecoming Court, the hotel loomed behind us.

At The Hacienda, I attended disco dances on Saturday nights and drank my first cocktail, a sloe gin fizz, while underage. In fact, I remember sobering up in the cool evening breeze by the fountain in the courtyard before driving my Datsun B-210 hatchback home to Tanglewood Terrace.

Shortly after graduation, I returned to The Hacienda as a groomsman—in a ruffled shirt, bow tie and burgundy tuxedo—in a wedding in the hotel's courtyard. I had the distinction of being chosen for the wedding party after a groomsman abruptly dropped out because I had the perfect build for the rented tuxedo that had already been altered for him.

After I graduated from college and became a licensed mental health counselor, the hotel retreated into my past as a dim memory. Then in 1994, my spouse and I sold our bungalow in Tampa's historic Seminole Heights and built a new home in New Port Richey. I frequently attended courses for continuing education credit at the former Hacienda Hotel. During presentations on psychotropic medications and cognitive behavioral therapy techniques, I became distracted by memories of dancing to music by A Flock of Seagulls and Dexys Midnight Runners in the lobby ballroom and ghost hunting on the spiritually active third floor.

On one sad day in the early twenty-first century, The Hacienda closed its doors. An entire generation knew the hotel as only an abandoned, boarded-up, derelict structure during the city's unfortunate decline. This was heartbreaking for those of us who were connected to the hotel's past and protective of its landmark status. Time after time, investors proposed its redevelopment, only to retreat, and the building continued to decay. I entertained fantasies of winning the Florida lottery and restoring The Hacienda to its former glory as a gift to the city. I envisioned an interior design theme involving each room being dedicated to one of the hotel's former famous guests and decorating each with vintage images of these individuals.

Repeated disappointment transformed into grateful elation when Jim Gunderson, a proverbial knight in shining armor, rescued The Hacienda from the wrecking ball by purchasing and restoring it as a private investment. As an experienced hotelier with a reverence for history and meticulous attention to detail, Gunderson was the perfect investor with an aspirational vision and the essential talent to save The Hacienda and spearhead a proper restoration. I am his number one fan.

When Oscar attended The Hacienda's gala opening with me in 2022, he fell in love with her, too. Having recently survived a heart attack and stroke, Oscar ended his career in corporate America as a division director and sought a new career with work-life balance. He suddenly envisioned himself working at The Hacienda.

The Monday following the gala, Oscar interviewed for a position at the hotel's front desk. Hotel manager Rafe Banks hired him on the spot, and Oscar is now the charming concierge in a fedora who greets guests every weekday afternoon and evening. My charismatic spouse is known as the ambassador of The Hacienda, where he provides brief historic tours.

Ironically, my spouse is now employed at the hotel, which I perceive as a significant part of *my* past. And the hotel's ghosts make known to him their appreciation for his caretaking.

In the spirit of local historian and educator Jeff Miller, I offer the remarkable story of the Hacienda Hotel, a living legend and New Port Richey's architectural crown jewel.

1

NEW PORT RICHEY'S RARE PINK LADY

"A Bit of Spain Among the Palms"

The Hacienda Hotel (1927), New Port Richey's architectural crown jewel, was conceived as a community hotel by northern developers on land donated by James E. Meighan, the brother of film star Thomas Meighan. Designed in the Mediterranean Revival style by prominent architect Thomas Reed Martin, the hotel hosted stage and screen actors, screenwriters, literati, composers, pop singers and sports figures such as Thomas Meighan, Raymond Hitchcock, Flora Zabelle, Dorothy Dalton, Ring Lardner, George Ade and Gene Sarazen. Originating from Great Neck, Long Island, where they easily commuted by rail to Broadway and the early motion picture studios in Queens, these winter "snowbirds" aspired to colonize a "Great Neck of the South" in Florida's warm, sunny climate.

The Hacienda flourished as a social and cultural center for civic meetings, lectures, weddings and proms as it became the topic of local lore related to the Prohibition era and the legendary actor Gloria Swanson. By the 1970s, the hotel served as a venue for musical performances by notables such as Johnny Cash, Tiny Tim, Guy Lombardo, Rudy Vallée and Frankie Lane. In the early 1990s, the building was repurposed as a psychiatric facility for geriatric patients before it fell into a decline and lay abandoned for nearly two decades. Rescued from the wrecking ball and restored to its original grandeur by Jim Gunderson, a private investor who restored the Lakeside Inn in Mount Dora, Florida, The Hacienda is now a historic boutique hotel ushering in the city's renaissance.

In the early twenty-first century, this iconic pink hotel, once advertised as "a bit of Spain among the palms," engendered intrigue, nostalgia and pride in the city's residents, many of whom organized Friends of The Hacienda, which raised funds to preserve the hotel's structural integrity as many proposals for redevelopment waxed and waned over the years. Despite the hotel's poignant history and significant context to the city, it stood in ruin, waiting for a visionary developer to appear like a knight in shining armor to rescue it from anticipated demolition and restore it back to glory.

The Hacienda is touted as "a bit of Spain among the palms." *Advertisement in the* New Port Richey Press, *West Pasco Historical Society.*

Declared a national landmark in 1997, The Hacienda remains one of Florida's rare, classic Pink Lady hotels of the Jazz Age—Mediterranean-style structures featuring stucco façades painted in coral or blush hues. The style's architectural elements include arched openings, red clay tile roofs and tower-like upper stories. The Hacienda is one of the smallest and most recently restored of the extraordinary Pink Ladies.

Florida's Vinoy Park Hotel opened its doors in downtown St. Petersburg on New Year's Eve in 1925. Designed in the Mediterranean Revival style by Henry L. Taylor, the resort overlooked Straub Park and the Vinoy Yacht Basin. The lobby soared twenty-five feet in height and featured a vaulted ceiling with hand-stenciled cypress beams and ornate chandeliers. Guests enjoyed a Pompeiian-themed ballroom and a two-story dining room filled with Georgian-inspired design aesthetics. Many powerful American families, such as the Pillsburys and the Fleischmanns, frequented the resort, and its other prominent guests included baseball legend Babe Ruth and U.S. presidents Calvin Coolidge and Herbert Hoover.

The Don CeSar Hotel on St. Petersburg Beach, designed by Henry H. Dupont with a blend of Mediterranean and Moorish elements, opened in January 1928. Worried that the magnificent 220-room "pink castle" would sink into the sand, DuPont designed a massive floating concrete pad and pyramid footings to serve as its foundation. The Don CeSar hosted writer F. Scott Fitzgerald, attorney Clarence Darrow, baseball legend Lou Gehrig and seven presidents from Franklin Delano Roosevelt to Barack Obama.

One had to travel far and wide to find another Pink Lady. The first may have been Bermuda's Hamilton Princess Hotel and Beach Club, standing since New Year's Day 1885, the year after Queen Victoria's daughter Louise, for whom the hotel is named, visited the island. The only non-Mediterranean-inspired of all the Pink Lady hotels, the "Pink Princess" offered long, shady verandas, a blue slate roof and four stories of opulent guest rooms, each equipped with gas lights, hot and cold running water and a five-inch mirror to allow hotel guests to primp. Its famous guests included Ian Fleming and his mentor, Sir William Stephenson, codenamed "Intrepid," who headed the Allied forces' Atlantic censorship station located in the hotel and inspired the former's James Bond novels. Mark Twain smoked cigars on the veranda while he signed autographs and recited poetry.

Across the globe in the South Pacific, the Matson Navigation Company opened the Royal Hawaiian Hotel, designed in the Spanish-Moorish style, in Waikiki, Honolulu, in February 1927 as a luxury resort for steamship passengers. Architects Whitney Warren and Charles Delevan Wetmore included stained-glass Art Deco chandeliers, cloth-corded telephones, mail chutes and cupolas resembling Spanish Mission–style bell towers. The resort was quickly dubbed the "Pink Palace of the Pacific," and its guests included President Franklin Roosevelt, Shirley Temple, Marilyn Monroe and Joe DiMaggio.

As one of these rare architectural and historical treasures, The Hacienda is the snuggest of all the Pink Ladies and the only one found in a relatively lightly populated city. Located in west-central Pasco County, charming New Port Richey encompasses a total area of 4.6 miles, bordered to the west by the Gulf of Mexico coastline, and is considered part of the Tampa Bay Area.

New Port Richey's rich history dates back millennia, when Indigenous people inhabited its lush, tropical land. It was first recorded in the nineteenth century, when pioneers settled and called their town Hickory Hammock and Hopeville.

2

HICKORY HAMMOCK, HOPEVILLE AND PORT RICHEY

The Origin of New Port Richey

T he area comprising New Port Richey in west Pasco County, Florida, was originally part of a town named Port Richey. Eventually, Port Richey was subdivided, and its southern region was named New Port Richey and incorporated in 1924. Its sister city, Port Richey, incorporated the following year. The Gulf of Mexico's coastline borders the west side of New Port Richey, and the meandering Pithlachascotee River, commonly known as the Cotee, traverses the historic downtown area. Residences and businesses developed along the river's shore and around Orange Lake.

New Port Richey's growth was affected by many social changes in Florida during the early twentieth century, notably the expansion of the railroad, the popularity of the automobile and the land boom of the 1920s. The area's sunshine and warm climate attracted many northerners to this city, nicknamed the "gateway to tropical Florida," and a group of entertainers, literati and sports legends from Great Neck, New York, transformed the city into the "Hollywood of the East" when they established a small winter enclave colony there. These affluent luminaries melded with the local townsfolk, descendants of early settlers and middle-class fellow transplants from northern states. Early developers promoted the city as a place for fishing, hunting, golfing, leisure and retirement, and early advertisements claimed the area offered an abundance of fish, oysters and game and attractive, dense, tropical foliage.

Centuries before the arrival of motion picture actors, authors and golf legends, Indigenous communities settled in the area comprising Port Richey and New Port Richey. Records document the first inhabitants before

10,000 BCE. The peaceful Timucua tribe thrived in the area during the 1200s, and when Spanish explorers arrived in the sixteenth century, they encountered numerous Native communities. These Indigenous residents had disappeared by the late 1700s, when fragments of tribes known as Seminoles from the southwest migrated to the area.

Early Settlers of Seven Springs

In 1830, Samuel H. Stevenson (1810–1897) and his wife, Elizabeth Osteen (1820–1900), first settled in what is now west Pasco County in an area they named Seven Springs, located just south of today's New Port Richey, along the Anclote River. Born in Canada, Stevenson seemingly did not exhibit documentation of his naturalization. On November 11, 1871, the *Florida Peninsular* reported that Stevenson attended the Taxpayers' Convention of Hernando County. Elizabeth served as a midwife and assisted in many births.

West Pasco County was part of Alachua County, soon to be part of Hernando County. Created in 1843 and named for Spanish explorer Hernando de Soto, Hernando County was renamed Benton County in 1844 in honor of Missouri senator Thomas Hart Benton (1782–1858), who urged Congress to pass the Armed Occupation Act. The bill's passing opened central west Florida to settlement and enabled Samuel H. Stevenson to acquire land near Clearwater. Most local Seminoles had been relocated to Oklahoma by the 1840s, when resettlement began under the Armed Occupation Act. In 1850, Benton County reverted to the name Hernando County due to Senator Benton's strong antislavery stand in a region where the citizens favored slavery.

Hickory Hammock, Also Known as Hopeville

Hopeville, established around 1850, was the first settlement in what would eventually become the original town of Port Richey and, later, New Port Richey. Hopeville also boasted the county's first post office. According to historian Frances Clark Mallett, Hopeville was named for members of the prominent Hope family in Hernando County. Brothers David and Henry Hope were involved in an operation that produced salt from salt springs in Hopeville for the Confederacy during the Civil War. During the Civil War, saltworks along the Gulf Coast were the principal suppliers of salt to the South.

Henry Hope Sr. (1810–1869) resided on 160 acres in the Spring Lake area at Chocochattee (or Chocochatti) that he purchased from his father-in-law, Michael Garrison. The land came from a grant that was a result of the Armed Occupation Act. Passed by Congress in 1842, the act allowed each settler—who cultivated five or more acres of land in eastern and southern Florida for a period of five years—to receive 160 acres of land from the federal government. Hope's land had been occupied by Upper Creek Natives from Alabama until President Andrew Jackson's Indian Removal Act of 1830 authorized the government to grant unsettled lands west of the Mississippi in exchange for Native lands within existing state borders.

In February 1883, the State of Florida sold to the Florida Land Improvement Company several hundred thousand acres of land located mainly in what are now Pinellas and Pasco Counties at twenty-five cents per acre. Part of the city of St. Petersburg and almost all of New Port Richey are currently located on these lands. By May 1883, the Florida Land Improvement Company had conveyed part of these lands, including the site of Port Richey, to Anson Peacely Killen Safford (1830–1891), the former governor of the Arizona Territory who had relocated to Florida and become involved with building the community of Tarpon Springs.

RICHEY POINT

In 1883, horticulturist and furniture dealer Aaron McLaughlin Richey (1837–1912) left St. Joseph, Missouri, to visit his friend James Washington Clark, who had left his land in Hickory Hammock (Hopeville) and settled forty miles northeast in Brooksville. In 1872, Clark and his wife, Fannie L. Hope, had established a home on the banks of the Pithlachascotee River on the Gulf of Mexico. Since Clark maintained his landholdings on the river, the two men traveled to this early settlement to benefit from its abundance in fishing and game.

While camping on Clark's property, Richey decided the warm climate and sunshine would benefit his ailing wife, Mary L. Richey (1832–1899), and their three minor children. Between June and July, Richey negotiated the purchase of a point of land at the mouth of the Pithlachascotee River owned by Felix Sowers and his wife, Martha Ann Bradshaw. Originally from

North Carolina, the Sowers arrived in Hopeville in 1879. Soon, the Richey family settled in a stone house on their newly purchased property.

Eyeing both commerce and transportation, Richey had a schooner built in Cedar Key. When the schooner was delivered, he thought it necessary to register the vessel in the name of its home port. Since the place where it would be moored did not have a name, Richey called it Richey Point.

On July 9, 1884, Richey founded a post office and named it Port Richey, signifying the beginning of the cities of Port Richey and New Port Richey.

PIONEERS OF NEW PORT RICHEY

In 1872, James Washington Clark (1838–1913) from South Carolina and his wife, Frances Louise Hope (1850–1915) of Brooksville, settled in what was then Hickory Hammock (not yet named Hopeville) on the mouth of the Pithlachascotee River, a hollow of dense palmetto palms where the couple raised cattle and citrus. They are the first known pioneer settlers in today's New Port Richey. Clark served as the first postmaster of the Hopeville Post Office, established in December 1878 and closed in 1881.

Shortly after James W. Clark settled here, Malcolm M. Hill, a native of Florida, arrived with his wife, Emma E. Hancock. The couple established a home on today's Massachusetts Avenue in New Port Richey. In 1904, Robert Nicks relocated from the Brooksville area to a large property on the Cotee River and married Latha Hope.

In January 1885, Anson Peacely Killen Safford conveyed his lands, including the current Port Richey and New Port Richey, to the Cooty Land Improvement Company. Subsequently, in 1887, Pasco County was formed with the passing of House Bill no. 305 and named after Samuel Pasco (1834–1917), a Confederate veteran, schoolmaster and U.S. senator from Florida. However, there is no evidence of Samuel Pasco visiting the county named in his honor.

THE SAWMILL ERA

In May 1897, the Cooty Land and Improvement Company sold Safford's former land to Sessions and Bullard, turpentine and timber operators. In

1905, Sessions and Bullard sold the 280,000 acres of land in West Pasco, Hillsborough and Hernando Counties to Aripeka Saw Mills, a Georgia corporation. An old sawmill on the property that had previously burned was included in the purchase. The area was known as Fivay Junction in west Pasco County.

The town of Fivay was named after five investors from Georgia whose last names began with the letter A: Gordon Abbott, M.F. Amorous, H.M. Atkinson, P.S. Arkright and Charles F. Ayer. After purchasing the large parcel of land, the men reopened and expanded a defunct sawmill and built the Tampa Northern Railroad. Eventually, they sold the land to recoup some of their investment, creating the catalyst that resulted in the future development of New Port Richey. The five investors had been involved in the Atlanta Street Railway and Electric enterprise, which later became Georgia Power Company, and some of them owned lumber interests in Georgia.

This partnership of five investors launched the new mill in 1905 and expanded to another. One mill cut pine off the lands, and the other cut cypress. These Aripeka Sawmills in Fivay were located fifteen miles from the current U.S. Highway 41 on a large millpond (created by damming Bear Creek, which led to Bear Sink, one hundred yards downstream) into which the logs were dumped. Investor Marin F. Amorous played the major role in overseeing the Aripeka Saw Mills operation.

Once the pine timber was depleted, the huge mill was closed, the railroad was dismantled and the workers relocated to other mill towns. When production ceased in 1912, the Aripeka Saw Mills ran an advertisement in *Tampa Daily Times* on March 2, offering the entire town of Fivay for sale, but there were no buyers.

ORIGINAL DEVELOPERS: WEEKS, WEEKS AND GUILFORD

In 1911, the Aripeka Saw Mills sold a part of its lands to P.L. Weeks, a turpentine still operator from Brooksville. In August that year, P.L. Weeks, his brother J.S. Weeks Jr. and W.E. Guilford (formerly of the Gillette Razor Blade Company) formed the Port Richey Company with the intention to colonize and develop the land into a townsite.

The Weeks brothers and Guilford drew the plan for their future town, but the streets and avenues they surveyed were unnamed. On August 16, 1911,

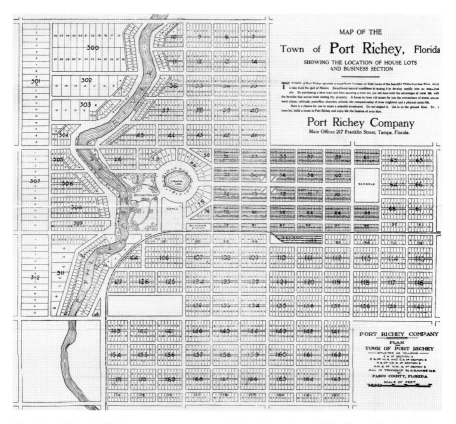

New Port Richey's 1911 plat map reserves a city block for a hotel. *West Pasco Historical Society.*

their map, titled *Port Richey Company Plan for Town of Port Richey*, with the city's first known layout was filed for record in plat book 1 on page 62. According to notations on the map, the partners maintained a "New England office" in Boston and a local office at 217 Franklin Street in downtown Tampa. An entire city block was reserved for a hotel.

The Port Richey Company's updated *Plan for the Town of Port Richey*, dated October 15, 1911, and officially filed the following day, was credited to S.A. Wheeler, a civil engineer from Port Richey, and Wayne E. Stiles, a landscape architect from Boston, Massachusetts. The area designated as a downtown business district was clustered around the intersection of the future Main Street, east to west, and future Grand Boulevard, north to south, which doglegged around a residential area surrounding Orange Lake and continued north along the east shore of the snaking Pithlachascotee River. The road around the lake was later named Circle Boulevard. The

Residences develop around Orange Lake, circa 1915. *West Pasco Historical Society.*

town's east-to-west avenues were later named after states, and its north-to-south streets were later named after presidents of the United States.

The Port Richey Company designated a large tract of land along the river for a town park, named Enchantment Park in the plan, stretching from today's Sims Lane south to Nebraska Avenue, encompassing today's Main Street and Hacienda Hotel property. A passenger railroad station was designated to the south and directly across from the hotel with a freight yard designated four blocks east. The railroad tracks traversed west and then curved southeast, parallel to the river over which it eventually crossed. Another large tract comprising two city blocks was designated for "schools."

Over the next two years, a financially distressed Pete L. Weeks and his partners offered to sell their fourteen thousand acres of semi-jungle along the bank of the Pithlachascotee River. According to advertisements from the Port Richey Company, a ten-dollar down payment would secure a lot: "Slip a $10 bill into an envelope and mail it to us today. You will be assigned the best unsold lot at the price you wish to pay."

"There is much activity at Port Richey, which, because of the development of the colony lands surrounding it, is beginning to take on a new life," reported the *Tampa Daily Times* on January 20, 1912. "The building of the railroad from Tarpon Springs to Port Richey, a distance of seven miles, also has much to do with the improvements now going on."

Early Downtown Development

To provide lodging for prospective land buyers from the North, the Weeks brothers planned to build and operate an inn. On January 20, 1912, the *Tampa Daily Times* reported on a "new hotel being erected by the Port Richey Company" on the Circle, south of Orange Lake, which was expected to be ready for guests by February 1. "It is a well-constructed frame building with wide verandas, [a] large office and dining room and ten or twelve bedrooms," the article announced. "The price for accommodations will be very low, the idea of the company being not to make money, but to provide a comfortable and inexpensive stopping place for land buyers who may desire to spend a few days looking over the Port Richey company's lands. As soon as the brick for the chimney arrives, the work will be finished."

On February 12, the *Tampa Daily Times* reported on the hotel's progress:

> *A force of workmen are engaged in erecting a well-designed hotel. Work has also been commenced on a new store which will be opened and occupied by Mr. W.R. McNatt, and a passenger station and freight warehouse is to go up at once. Several residences and storehouses are in prospect. To ensure the rapid upbuilding of Port Richey, the Port Richey Company is giving absolutely free to each purchaser of a ten-acre farm tract a lot in the town. The majority of purchasers will build on their free town lots, and thus, the rapid growth of Port Richey is assured.*

Fred Sass purchased Pete Weeks's hotel before its completion. Known over the next fourteen years as the Sass Hotel, the Inn and Enchantment Inn, the business served as the social center of the fledgling community and

The Enchantment Inn, the city's first hotel overlooking Orange Lake that was later known as the Sass Hotel, burned in a dramatic fire in 1926. *West Pasco Historical Society.*

Top: First State Bank opened on the northwest corner of Grand Boulevard and Main Street in 1921. *West Pasco Historical Society.*

Second: City pioneer James William Clark Jr.'s two-story brick mercantile building opened on the southwest corner of Grand Boulevard and Main Street. Known as the Clark building, it was considered a modern, fireproof structure with electric lighting and running water. *West Pasco Historical Society.*

Third: Built in 1915, the Havens building on Main Street housed Emil Nyman's Standard Grocery, a woodworking shop, the post office and, later, the Hotel Rialto. In 1925, Mort S. Swafford purchased the building, and the following year, the brick Swafford building replaced the original wooden structure. *West Pasco Historical Society.*

Bottom: The view facing south at the intersection of Grand Boulevard and Main Street, circa 1926. *West Pasco Historical Society.*

26

changed hands once but soon returned to the ownership of Sass. It burned to the ground in the spring of 1926, shortly before the grand opening of the Hacienda Hotel.

Railroad Services Hastens Development

On August 16, 1912, *Railway Age Gazette* reported, "A new branch has been opened for freight service only from Tarpon Springs, Fla., to Port Richey, eight miles. C.H. Lutz, secretary, treasurer and general manager, Odessa, Fla." A small train depot in town was completed in November 1912 on land that is now the northeast corner of Grand Boulevard and Nebraska Avenue. The building of the railroad bridge across the Pithlachascotee River near Lafayette Street delayed the arrival of trains until the summer of 1913, when semi-weekly train service was established.

Port Richey Land Company Sells

According to Dr. Elroy M. Avery, New Port Richey's first mayor, P.L. Weeks grew weary of his land sales endeavor. "Mr. Weeks soon tired of pouring money into a proposition where everything went out, and nothing seemed to be coming in," the mayor recalled. "[Business partner] Mr. Guilford, with cooling ardor and the impatience of all real dreamers, departed for other fields. He had reached first base but had not made a home run. It required perspiration as well as inspiration to make a real town here."

In February 1913, P.L. Weeks sold his holdings to Brooksville Hammock Land Company, owned by George Reginald Sims and R.E. Filcher, who formed the New Port Richey Land Corporation, differentiating it from the Weeks brothers' Port Richey Company. With this changing of the guard, a new momentum invigorated the town's development.

The new owners, with an office on Zack Street in Tampa, advertised "the price of our lots range from $100 to $500 per lot, but to anyone who will build in one year, we will give a lot 50x100 feet in the heart of the townsite absolutely free—come and help make us make Port Richey the metropolis of the West Coast."

Enter George Reginald Sims, the founding father of New Port Richey.

GEORGE REGINALD SIMS

*The Founding Father of New Port Richey Paves the Way
for the Hacienda Hotel*

George Reginald Sims (1876–1954), known as "Reg," was the third son of Walter Sims and Elizabeth Knowles Sims. He was born on September 5, 1876, shortly after the family relocated from Hamilton, Ontario, to Detroit, Michigan. By the time Reg was two, he and his family had relocated to Bay City, Michigan, where Walter Sims became a lay preacher and newspaper editor.

In 1895, George R. Sims entered the University of Michigan. Apparently, he never graduated. In 1923, the university listed him in the general catalogs as having attended from 1895 to 1896 and from 1897 to 1898 under the category of "non-graduate."

By 1900, Sims lived in Woodlawn, a southside suburb of Chicago, near his brother Edwin. Joined by his brother Harry and another nonrelative partner, Sims established the mail order company Sims, Wilson and Sims. When the business went bankrupt in 1903, Sims relocated to New York City, where he served as the president of the University Publishing Company, a publisher of textbooks.

With his brother Harry as a groomsman, Sims married Marjorie Bartlett Byington (1884–1965), known as Bess, in a home wedding in Memphis, Tennessee, on March 1, 1904. Marjorie and her parents had relocated from Chicago to Tennessee for health reasons. She was described in the *Chicago Inter Ocean* as "one of the daintiest and prettiest South Side [Chicago] girls and cross-country riders we have among the girls—and that is saying much,

George Reginald Sims (1976–1954). *West Pasco Historical Society.*

for many of them out-ride the men." The couple's son, George Reginald "Blunt" Sims, was born in Manhattan on May 13, 1906.

The Simses spent their summer months in a secondary residence in Great Neck, Long Island, where they befriended motion picture actors, a professional golfer and literati who maintained estates in the area. This social networking featured prominently in the early development of New Port Richey as a winter haven for entertainers and celebrities. Great Neck and its Kings Point community later provided a backdrop to F. Scott Fitzgerald's novel *The Great Gatsby* and symbolized the Roaring Twenties Jazz Era as entertainment personalities purchased residences in the hamlet.

By 1910, the Sims family had returned to Chicago, where Reg became involved in property development. He formed the Pellston Farm Land company with Ralph E. Filcher of California. Filcher graduated from Stanford University in 1899 and achieved a California license to practice law. Filcher had invested heavily in San Francisco real estate (from 1900 to 1908) and relocated to Chicago around 1909.

Sims's Investment in New Port Richey

While investing in Michigan property, Sims and Filcher formed Filcher and Sims Real estate, a company based in Tampa, Florida. In 1911, they acquired the Brooksville Hammock Land Company, a corporation intent on developing land in Hernando County, Florida, about forty-five miles northeast of Tampa.

According to the *Orlando Sentinel*, on February 25, 1913, with Sims and Filcher still based in Chicago, their Brooksville Hammock Land Company acquired the Port Richey Land Company from P.L. Weeks. Acquired for $300,000, the land was originally part of a thirty-thousand-acre parcel in Pasco County that surrounded the towns of Port Richey, Hudson and Fivay, the latter having been the site of a sawmill.

On May 9, 1913, the *Tarpon Springs Leader* reported that Sims and Filcher purchased the Port Richey Company and its lands, including the townsite of Port Richey on April 1.

By 1916, Sims had acquired Filcher's interest in the company, becoming the president and sole owner of the New Port Richey Land Corporation. Filcher returned to California to develop land in Los Angeles, and Sims served as "developer, cheerleader and booster" for New Port Richey,

George Reginald Sims, the "father of New Port Richey," poses with his family (*left to right*): his wife, Marjorie Bartlett Byington Sims; his son, George "Blunt" Reginald Sims II; and his mother-in-law, Sallie Byington. *Published in the* New Port Richey Press, *January 12, 1922; West Pasco Historical Society.*

according to his descendants. Sims started a chamber of commerce, built commercial buildings and fostered many civic organizations. Filcher died on July 21, 1929, in Los Angeles.

With their son Bunt in boarding school in New York and later at Mercersburg College Preparatory School in Pennsylvania, George and Marjorie started the construction of a residence on their land between the Old Dixie Highway and the Pithlachascotee River. On December 29, 1915, the *Tampa Morning Tribune* reported on the erection of the couple's bungalow. They continued to spend their summers in Great Neck, Long Island, where they befriended motion picture actor Thomas Meighan and his wife, Frances Ring Meighan, who, along with Meighan's brother, featured heavily in the development of the Hacienda Hotel.

George and Marjorie's original residence in New Port Richey remains at the intersection of Grand Boulevard and Queen's Lane, the latter reportedly named for Marjorie, who held the title of the first Queen Chasco of an annual community Chasco Fiesta, first held in 1922. "[My wife] favored the site where we now live," Sims wrote in 1922, "but I maintained that was entirely too far out of town. We argued the matter for several days, and finally compromised by building the bungalow where she wanted it."

By 1914, the area around Orange Lake was commonly called New Port Richey, and the older part of Port Richey was called Old Port Richey. On July 14, 1914, a newspaper article referred to "old Port Richey" and "new Port Richey," and school board minutes also used both names in July 1914. By 1915, a separate post office had been established for the residents of the southern part of Port Richey and was named New Port Richey, making the name official.

SIMS CATAPULTS DEVELOPMENT

On December 27, 1915, Sims's New Port Richey Company filed for record a *Revised Plan for Town of New Port Richey* in plat book 2 on page 21. The city's second layout included the name of the newly established post office. Glaring changes to the original plan filed in 1911 by the Weeks brothers and Guilford included the loss of lands designated for a school, a rail freight yard, a train depot, a city hall, a library, a bank and a theater. Additionally, Sims's revision reduced by nearly half the size of the town's previously designated Enchantment Park. The southern half of Enchantment Park was now reserved as "Block B, for Hotel."

George R. Sims donated the land that contained Enchantment Park (currently Sims Park) to the city in 1924. *West Pasco Historical Society.*

Sims Land Company, located on the southeast corner of Grand Boulevard and Main Street, has the distinction of being the city's first brick building, completed in 1919. *West Pasco Historical Society.*

On October 27, 1924, residents voted 201 to 4 in favor of incorporating New Port Richey and elected Dr. Elroy M. Avery the town's first mayor. On May 18, 1925, Governor John W. Martin signed the special legislative act creating the incorporated town of Port Richey.

On the same day of the incorporation of New Port Richey, Sims had the southern section of the park, designated as "Block B, for Hotel," surveyed into several smaller lots, as recorded in plat book 2, page 46.

Ordinance 1

On November 14, 1924, the *New Port Richey Press* published a lengthy letter by Sims that announced his intention to grant the park to the newly appointed city council, subject to several restrictions, including the nullification of the 1911 plat designating a larger park.

On November 18, 1924, city leaders accepted Sims's gift with restrictions and obligations. On December 2, 1924, the gift was formally received through the unanimous passing of City Ordinance no. 1. On the recommendation of an appreciative Mayor Elroy Avery, the grateful city council also changed the name of Enchantment Park to Sims Park. However, this donation of land was not without controversy. The cancellation of the original plats gave Sims legal control of undeveloped land previously designated as part of the park and permitted an extension of Main Street, where a hotel could be built. Today, the business Ordinance One is a brewery in a space on Main Street that once housed the New Port Richey Fire Department.

Sims in Later Years

George Sims's prominence extended to surrounding areas. He served as the director of the First National Bank, Fort Myers, and maintained a membership with the Masons, the Tampa Yacht and Country Club, the Palma Ceia Golf Club and the Tarpon Springs Golf Club.

On May 24, 1954, George Sims died suddenly of a stroke at the age of seventy-seven at his home on the shores of the Pithlachascotee River, where he and Marjorie had lived for nearly four decades. The couple had returned home the previous day from a visit to see George's brother William Sims in Miami. His brother Hubert had died in Tampa in February while spectating the annual Gasparilla Parade. The founding father of New Port Richey commanded a two-column obituary that included his photograph in the *Tampa Tribune*.

As the founding father of New Port Richey, Sims was buried in downtown New Port Richey about fifty feet from the north end of Orange Lake. His grave site has no tombstone, just a redbud tree to mark the location of the land he had donated to the city.

At the age of seventy-seven, on March 4, 1965, Marjorie died at Tarpon Springs Hospital. Marjorie's obituary referred to her as the "first lady of New Port Richey" and said she was a renowned "gracious and charming hostess." George Sims's remains were exhumed and interred next to those of his wife in Sylvan Abbey Memorial Park on Curlew Road in Clearwater.

4

THE HACIENDA

An Icon of the Jazz Age

The Hacienda Hotel stands as an icon of the 1920s, an era referred to as the Roaring Twenties and the Jazz Age. As residents of New Port Richey prepared for the hotel's opening gala in the rapidly developing city, the nation experienced dramatic social, economic and political changes. For the first time, more Americans lived in cities than on farms, and the nation's total wealth more than doubled during the decade.

Increased financial prosperity contributed to Americans' disposable income, which they spent on entertainment and conveniences. This combination of cash and technological advancements produced new patterns of leisure and consumption. Washing machines, vacuum cleaners and refrigerators became everyday household items.

Educated and skilled Americans now received paid vacations, pensions and fringe benefits, affording them the luxuries of travel and investment in real estate. With the prosperous economy, credit was easy to acquire if one had a decent job. In this new economic environment, those who desired to make money by selling land swarmed into Florida. Known as land speculators, they purchased land at low prices and sold at a large profit.

During what was called the Florida land boom, most people who bought and sold land in Florida had never even set foot in the state. Instead, they hired ambitious salesmen to show the land to prospective buyers and accept a binder on the sale. The binder was a nonrefundable down payment that required the balance of the sale price to be paid in thirty days. With land prices rising rapidly, many of the buyers planned to sell the land at a profit before the real land payments were due.

The 1920s ushered in the first generation of motion picture stars: Charles Chaplin, Douglas Fairbanks, Rudolph Valentino, Thomas Meighan, Mary Pickford, Lillian Gish, Marion Davies and Gloria Swanson. Radio and magazines catapulted film actors and athletes into national celebrity status. Babe Ruth dominated baseball. Gene Sarazen personified golf.

An archetype of the '20s was the "flapper," a young woman with bobbed hair and a short skirt who challenged social norms by wearing excessive cosmetics, drinking alcohol, smoking cigarettes in public, driving automobiles and speaking in "unladylike" ways. More concerning to those of the more conservative Victorian and Edwardian eras, these young women were more sexually disinhibited than women from previous generations. However, most young women of the time, especially those who lived in small, conservative cities, adopted the fashionable flapper hairstyles and wardrobe but did not engage in flapper-like behavior.

Overall, women generally gained unprecedented freedoms beginning in 1920, when the Nineteenth Amendment to the U.S. Constitution legally guaranteed American women the right to vote after decades of agitation and protest.

Under the Eighteenth Amendment, Prohibition prevented the manufacture, sale and transportation of alcoholic beverages in the United States from 1920 to 1933. Although the widely accepted temperance movement had succeeded

East view of Main Street at the intersection of Grand Boulevard. *Published in the* New Port Richey Press, *March 4, 1927; West Pasco Historical Society.*

in bringing about this legislation, millions of Americans were willing to drink liquor illegally, giving rise to the illegal production and sale of liquor (bootlegging) and illegal, secret drinking establishments (speakeasies), both controlled by organized crime.

The decade's musical sound ranged from George Gershwin's melding of classical music and jazz in "Rhapsody in Blue" to the raucous jazz standard "Sweet Georgia Brown." The era's popular recording artists included Helen Kane, Ruth Etting, Annette Hanshaw, Bessie Smith and Al Jolson. Crooner Rudy Vallée became the first vocal superstar of the century. His popular songs included "Baby Face," "If You Knew Susie (Like I Know Susie)," "Button Up Your Overcoat" and "Happy Days Are Here Again."

New dance crazes exemplified the change in social norms and sexual expression. The smooth and graceful foxtrot of the early 1920s gave way to the Charleston, which could be performed by both solo dancers and couples. The tango migrated from South America, with its overtly sensual moves described as a "walking embrace." Frenetically syncopated rhythms inspired dances such as the black bottom and Texas Tommy.

Built in 1926–27, the Hacienda Hotel, architect Thomas Reed Martin's graceful and sumptuously detailed structure, embodies the American optimism of the Jazz Age and remains a prime example of the era's Mediterranean Revival design.

5

NEW PORT RICHEY

The Great Neck, Long Island, of the South

George Reginald Sims invited his renowned social network in Great Neck, Long Island, to New Port Richey, commanding a modern, sumptuous hotel for their accommodation. Although the Enchantment Inn, Hotel Newport and Chasco Inn (then known as Harmony Hotel) successfully catered to middle-class northerners speculating investment in local property, these establishments could not offer the opulent venue a more sophisticated demographic demanded for lodging and later for social and cultural events. The market for what the Hacienda Hotel would soon provide was imminently approaching.

Great Neck is a region of Long Island, New York, that covers a peninsula on the North Shore and includes nine villages, among them Great Neck, Great Neck Estates, Great Neck Plaza and Kings Point. Located on the Great Neck Peninsula, Kings Point is a village in the town of North Hempstead in Nassau County, on the North Shore of Long Island, overlooking Long Island Sound.

During the 1910s, the ideal juxtaposition of metropolis and countryside attracted many prominent stage and screen personalities to Great Neck, spreading theatrical activities throughout the community. The area was a relatively short train ride to Manhattan's Broadway theaters or Queens's motion picture studios. In fact, the Long Island Railroad ran an 11:18 p.m. theater special for commuting actors.

Why Were Motion Picture Superstars Ensconced in Long Island and Not in Hollywood?

Film producer Adolph Zukor opened Astoria Studios in Queens, Long Island, in 1920 for the Famous Players Film Company, which merged into Famous Players–Lasky and, later, Paramount Pictures, which currently dominates the market. According to Marian Caballo, author of "Hollywood at Home: Cinema History in Queens, New York City," in *Science Survey* (April 27, 2022), following Thomas Edison and William Kennedy Dickson's invention of the kinetograph/kinetoscope in a New Jersey laboratory, the East Coast film industry flourished, with Astoria serving as "Mecca of the silent era." "It's convenient proximity to the Broadway theater district drew many creatives to the area," wrote Caballo, "and they produced over 100 films throughout the 1920s."

Astoria Studios became the home base of legendary actors who became the most popular talents of the silent film era, including Gloria Swanson, sisters Dorothy and Lillian Gish, Clara Bow, Gary Cooper, Rudolph Valentino and Thomas Meighan. Caballo wrote of the period yet a few years in the future, "However, the end of the silent era and Great Depression uncertainty sparked rapid transformation as the industry shifted from the East Coast to the West Coast."

Great Neck's Roster of the Rich and Famous

Jazz Age author F. Scott Fitzgerald and his wife, Zelda, lived at 6 Gateway Drive in Great Neck Estates, where they "struggled" on an annual salary of $36,000 while Fitzgerald wrote *The Great Gatsby*. He incorporated much of Great Neck's raucous social scene in the novel. Although the community's residents led relatively quiet lives, the area's theatrical enclave had a reputation for lively soirées.

According to *This Is Great Neck*, published by the League of Women Voters of Great Neck in 1983, during the early twentieth century, Great Neck boasted what was probably the highest number of nationally known personalities in a community of its size in America. Between 1912 and 1925, business property in the area soared in value by 3,000 percent.

Great Neck's residents were a who's who of stage, film and literature—and many became guests of the Hacienda Hotel and winter residents of New Port Richey:

Thomas Meighan and his wife, **Frances Ring**, a stage and film actor and a stage actor (in the Grenwolde section); **George Sims**, a land developer, and his wife, **Marjorie Byington** (on Sunset Road); **Raymond Hitchcock** and his wife, **Flora Zabelle**, stage and screen actors (on Sunset Road); **Earl Benham**, an actor-composer-tailor, and his wife, **Christine Mangasarian**, an actor (on Stoner Avenue); **Gene Sarazen**, a professional golfer; **Oscar Hammerstein II**, a composer, and his wife, **Dorothy Dalton**, a film actor (in Kennilworth); **Ed Wynn**, a radio and film actor and comedian, whose estate, Wynngate, was sold in 1920 for $400,000; **Ring Lardner**, a sports columnist, short story writer and screenwriter (on East Shore Road); **Ernest Truex**, a stage and film actor (on Vista Drive); **Nicholas Schenck**, a film studio executive, and his wife, **Norma Talmadge**, a film actor (in the Grenwolde section); **Sam Warner**, the cofounder or Warner Brothers Studios; **F. Scott Fitzgerald**, a novelist (on Gateway Drive); **Lillian Russell**, a stage actor; **Fredric March**, a film actor, and his wife, **Florence Eldridge**, a stage and film actor; **Sam H. Harris**, a Broadway producer and theater owner (on Sunset Drive at Elm Point); the **Marx brothers**, a film comedy act (Groucho lived on Lincoln Road); **George M. Cohan**, the great actor, playwright and songwriter, lived in a breathtaking hilltop home at the corner of Steppingstone Lane and Kings Point Road.

Literary humorist Ring Lardner, a Great Neck resident, often included satirical observations of his neighbors in his syndicated contributions to national newspapers. "Great Neck is something of a literary and theatrical center," he wrote in 1927, and then he proceeded with wisecracks about Great Neck's famous inhabitants who were his closest friends. Lardner referred to Ed Wynn as a "female impersonator," Raymond Hitchcock as a "soft shoe hoofer" and Ernest Truex as "the bridge authority." When referencing Thomas Meighan, Lardner wrote, "Is it a man or wolf?" When the Marx brothers and Eddie Cantor purchased homes in the neighborhood, Lardner revealed, "Neither of them had come anywhere close to paying cash."

When F. Scott Fitzgerald and Zelda spent time in Europe, journalist Ring Lardner kept them abreast of the social shenanigans in Great Neck through

Summer residents of Great Neck, New York, socialize at the Hacienda Hotel during their winter residency in New Port Richey, circa January 1928. *Left to right*: Marjorie Byington Sims (Mrs. George Sims); Flora Zabelle (Mrs. Raymond Hitchcock); Frances Ring (Mrs. Thomas Meighan); Gene Sarazen; Christine Mangasarian Benham (Mrs. Earl Benham and Zabelle's sister); George Reginald Sims; Mary Peck Sarazen (Mrs. Gene Sarazen); and Earl Benham. *West Pasco Historical Society.*

warm, descriptive letters. In one letter, published by Matthew J. Bruccoli, the satirical writer mentioned his neighbors Ed Wynn, Blanche Ring and Thomas Meighan:

> *On the Fourth of July, Ed Wynn gave a fireworks party at his new estate in the Grenwolde division. After the children had been sent home, everybody got pie-eyed and I never enjoyed a night so much. All the Great Neck professionals did their stuff, the former chorus girls danced, Blanche Ring kissed me and sang, etc. The party lasted through the next day and wound up next evening at Tom Meighan's, when the principal entertainment was provided by Lila Lee and another dame, who did some very funny imitations (really funny) in the moonlight on the tennis court.*

Left to right: Marjorie Byington Sims (Mrs. George Sims); Frances Ring (Mrs. Thomas Meighan); Gene Sarazen; George Reginald Sims (*in plaid shirt and hat*); Flora Zabelle (Mrs. Raymond Hitchcock, *seated*); Earl Benham; Christine Mangasarian Benham (Mrs. Earl Benham and Zabelle's sister); and Mary Peck Sarazen (Mrs. Gene Sarazen). *West Pasco Historical Society, restored by No Naked Walls Art and Frame Shop.*

In its January 3, 1926 issue, the *Tampa Sunday Tribune* reported on the *New Port Richey Press* having extended New Year's greetings to its readers and expressed pride in welcoming "famous men and women of American stage and concert platform" who had reportedly made purchases of house lots in the city. "The residence of these famous people in our beautiful town is the basis of a theatrical colony which will enable New Port Richey to boast of becoming the Great Neck of the South," the article predicted, "and in case it is news to some, Great Neck is the most popular Long Island habitat of the famous folk of the stage.…New Port Richey is fortunate in extending the glad-hand to its new residents.…The celebrated newcomers are to be congratulated upon their choice of a winter resort."

So, for a time, New Port Richey became the Great Neck of the South.

6

THOMAS MEIGHAN

Leading Motion Picture Actor, New Port Richey's Golden Boy and "Miracle Man" Brings Stage and Screen Luminaries and Literati to the City

Unless you're a silent motion picture aficionado, the name Thomas Meighan (1879–1936) may mean nothing to you. If you are a resident of New Port Richey, you may have no idea that Meighan was once the city's most renowned resident. A century ago, every resident of the city—as well as every American—knew the name and recognized the face of Thomas Meighan. He appeared in eighty-four motion pictures from 1914 to 1934.

Thoms Meighan was the Tom Cruise of the Jazz Age.

MEIGHAN ARRIVES IN NEW PORT RICHEY

On New Year Day, 1926, *New Port Richey Press* reported:

> FAMOUS MILLIONAIRES OF BROADWAY BUY IN NEW PORT RICHEY
> *Thomas Meighan and Paul Whiteman, Irving Berlin, Sam H. Harris Among Celebrities Who Have Purchased Here*
>
> *Celebrities famous the world over, owners of names as familiar to Paris theatre-goers and Australian music-lovers as they are to the inhabitants of old Manhattan Isle, have bought land in New Port Richey, and plan to build winter homes in this famous resort-town, the* New Port Richey Press *has learned. Recent purchases of building lots in this city, when*

generally known, will thrust New Port Richey in the public eye as no other community of like size in the limits of Florida can possibly be subjected to the calcium glare of publicity.

The New Port Richey Press *today as its New Year's greetings to its thousands of readers announces with warranted pride that a neighborly welcome in the next few months may be extended to the following famous men and Women of the American stage and concert platform; that the persons to be named in this story have already made bona-fide purchases of house lots in this vicinity; that the residence of these famous people in our beautiful town is the basis of a theatrical colony which will enable New Port Richey to boast of becoming the Great Neck of the South—(and in case it is new to some, Great Neck is the most popular Long Island habitat of the famous folk of the stage); that New Port Richey is fortunate in extending the glad-hand to its new residents and that the celebrated newcomers are to be congratulated upon their choice of a winter resort.*

Without more ado, here is the list of purchasers of home-sites in New Port Richey:

Thomas Meighan, Irving Berlin [composer and lyricist], *Paul Whiteman* [composer and bandleader], *Raymond Hitchcock* [stage and screen actor], *Leon Errol* [stage and screen comedian], *Blanche Ring* [stage and screen actor], *Sam H. Harris* [Broadway theatrical producer], *Charlotte Greenwood* [stage and screen actor and dancer], *Joseph Santley* [film producer for Paramount Pictures], *Earl Benham* [stage actor, composer, costumer and tailor].

Thomas Meighan, who for the past five years has stood pre-eminent as the he-man type of film hero, has purchased a water-front site within the city limits and a home in accord with his desires has been designed by a prominent New York architect and is to be begun as soon as the star's brother, James Meighan, returns to New Port Richey next week. Mrs. Meighan will accompany the famous Thomas on a trip to this city within a fortnight.

In his sprawling obituary in the *New York Times*, published on July 9, 1936, Thomas Meighan was eulogized as the motion picture industry's most popular leading man for more than a decade. For fifteen years before his

Opposite: Thomas Meighan (1879–1936). *PICRYL public domain archive, Get Archive LLC (public domain)*.

Right: Thomas Meighan in *The Bachelor Father* (1922, Famous Players-Lasky Corporation). *PICRYL public domain archive, Get Archive LLC (public domain)*.

global fame, Meighan "had come fairly close to the not always enviable rating of 'matinee idol' on the stage."

From 1914 to 1927, Meighan "was one of the cinema's top men, both in record of box-office success and popular vote," asserted the *New York Times*, and although his popularity declined after the advent of talking films, this "may have been due in part to his decision to go into the real estate business in Florida, which began booming just about that time." Meighan apparently had more retirements and comebacks than Cher. He appeared in fewer films after 1927 and then retired in 1929, returned in 1931, retired once more in 1932 and then came back in 1934 with a film "that proved he still was a box office 'draw' and a name to conjure with."

Born on April 9, 1879, in Pittsburgh to affluent parents, Meighan refused to attend college and was sent to work shoveling coal. After a week of heavy labor, the fifteen-year-old consented to study pharmacology at Mount St. Mary's College. After three years, Meighan abandoned medicine and joined the Pittsburgh Stock Company as an actor earning thirty-five dollars per week for two seasons. He appeared in *The Dictator* and *The Two Orphans* and had a leading role in *The College Widow*, which succeeded on Broadway in 1907–8.

In the stock company, Meighan met and fell in love with Frances Ring (1882–1951) while performing in the London engagement of George Ade's *The College Widow* in 1907. Frances was the sister of popular RCA recording artist and Broadway actor Blanche Ring, whose rendition of "Yip, Aye Addy, Aye Ay!" attracted considerable attention, and vaudeville and film actor Julie Ring. Frances Ring's Internet Broadway Database Credit begins with *The Bold Sojer Boy* in 1903 and ends with George M. Cohan's musical *Get-Rich-Quick Wallingford* in 1910.

Frances Ring became Mrs. Thomas Meighan in 1909, and the couple's marriage lasted until Meighan's death, prompting a columnist to remark, "Thomas Meighan and Rin Tin Tin were the only Hollywood stars who had never seen a divorce court." (Rin Tin Tin was a canine film performer.)

By 1914, Meighan had left the stage for the fledgling motion picture industry and appeared in the British film *Dandy Donovan, the Gentleman Cracksman*. This led him to have a contract with Famous Players–Lasky Corporation, which had studios in Astoria, New York. By 1916, Famous Players–Lasky had merged with Paramount Pictures, becoming the largest motion picture studio of its day.

In his first American film, *The Fighting Hope* (1915), Meighan played opposite character actor Laura Hope Crew, best remembered as Aunt Pittypat Hamilton in *Gone with the Wind* (1939). Soon after, Meighan achieved cinematic success in an iconic performance in *The Miracle Man* (1919), starring Lon Chaney, a film with which his name would be associated but of which only three minutes exist today. Director Cecil B. DeMille's *Male and Female* (1919) followed, costarring Gloria Swanson. Meighan went on to costar with Swanson in two other films for Paramount Studios.

Meighan peaked in popularity from 1916 to 1926, performing with leading ladies such as Billie Burke, Norma Talmadge, Mary Pickford and Louise Brooks and in films directed by Cecil B. DeMille. His highest weekly salary reported was $10,000. Meighan's final silent films, produced by Howard Hughes in 1928, were *The Mating Call*, critical of the Ku Klux Klan, and *The Racket*, nominated for an Academy Award for Best Picture.

By the late 1910s, Meighan's earnings had afforded him a massive waterfront estate on Grenwolde Drive in Great Neck, Long Island, with its own forty-foot-long pier. It was located next door to Wyngate, comedian Ed Wynn's estate. Meighan's residence was a short commute from Astoria Studios, where he filmed motion pictures. Thomas and Frances retained the property after becoming Florida winter "snowbirds," and today, it is part of the U.S. Merchant Marine Academy.

Thomas Meighan and Frances Ring Meighan enjoyed winters at Casa Francesca at Jasmin Point, New Port Richey. *West Pasco Historical Society*.

Rudolph Valentino, Gloria Swanson and Thomas Meighan were a Famous Players–Lasky Corporation Paramount Pictures trifecta of popularity, and they all ranked in the annual Top Ten Money Making Stars Poll, with standards set by the Quigley Publishing Company to determine the bankability of movie stars. How did Meighan compare to industry favorites Gloria Swanson, Rudolph Valentino, Mary Pickford and Douglas Fairbanks? He ranked fourth in 1922 (ahead of Valentino), first in 1923, fifth in 1924, tenth in 1925 and ninth in 1926, before falling off the list.

At Famous Players–Lasky Corporation in New York, Meighan barely knew fellow contracted employee Rudolph Valentino, an Italian-born actor idolized as the "great lover" or the "Latin lover" who redefined male sexuality. In May 1922, Valentino was arrested on a felony bigamy charge for having allegedly—and impulsively— married actor Natacha Rambova (whose legal name was Winifred Hudnut) in Mexico before his divorce from actor Jean Acker had become final. Allegedly, the marriage to Acker was never consummated. After submitting himself for arrest, Valentino was released on $10,000 bail, which was raised by June Mathis, a screenwriter; George Melford, a director; and Thomas Meighan. Reportedly, Meighan came to the rescue by selling his gold coin collection.

Gloria Swanson and Thomas Meighan costarred together in films released by Paramount Studios. *PICRYL public domain archive, Get Archive LLC (public domain).*

When Meighan's first sound feature film *The Argyle Case* (1928) was released, the actor was nearing fifty years of age. Anticipating waning popularity due to his aging, Meighan embarked on real estate ventures in Florida but then returned to the screen in *Young Sinners* (1931).

According to Meighan's obituary, beginning in 1925, he "became obsessed with Florida after talks with his realtor brother James E. Meighan." James had spent the winter of 1925–26 in New Port Richey, where he owned considerable property. According to the *New Port Richey Press*, James Meighan represented a syndicate that included his brother Thomas; Gloria Swanson, an actor and costar of Thomas; Victor Heerman, a film director; Nathan Burkan, a copyright lawyer and a founder of the American Society of Composers; and other celebrities associated with New York theatre.

In 1925, Thomas Meighan purchased property in Ocala, Florida, about one hundred miles northeast of New Port Richey, and his opportunities in Florida's booming real estate market distracted him from motion pictures. What brought Meighan to Ocala?

In 1917, Meighan's employer, Famous Players–Lasky Corporation (later Paramount Pictures), filmed many of its films' interior shots at its Astoria Studios on Long Island. Paramount's feature *It's the Old Army Game*, starring

Louise Brooks, was in production in February and March 1926 (when Thomas Meighan was visiting New Port Richey), and many of its exteriors were shot in Ocala.

By 1925, during the Florida real estate boom, a group of Ocala's leaders had planned a luxury community hotel to lure northern investors to the city. New luxurious lodgings seemed necessary to compete with other opulent Florida hotels, built by Henry Flagler on the east coast or Henry B. Plant in the Tampa Bay area, and to accommodate anticipated growth. A group formed an organization to raise the necessary money, and one of the investors was Thomas Meighan, who purportedly inspired local leaders with his predictions that Ocala could become a national center for filmmaking if it only had a suitable hotel. Meighan also joined with others to build the Ritz Apartments, Ocala's first apartment complex, and the Ritz Theatre, a cinema with a stage for live performances.

When Meighan and his brother James ventured south to New Port Richey, the charming rural town lured the actor from Ocala. Reportedly, Meighan and his brother purchased property in New Port Richey from Earl Benham, the actor, costumer and tailor who had invested in land as early as 1913, the year George Sims purchased the Port Richey Company. Benham's wife, actor Christine Mangasarian, was a sister of stage and screen actor Flora Zabelle, the wife of Raymond Hitchcock, a stage and screen comedian. The Hitchcocks, who owned an estate in Kings Point, Long Island, wintered in New Port Richey at the Hacienda Hotel and eventually purchased riverfront property.

The first official mention of Meighan visiting New Port Richey appeared on February 26, 1926, when the *New Port Richey Press* published a photograph of the actor with others. The headline ran, "Famous Film Hero Buys Land and Goes on a New Port Richey Picnic." His companions included Frances Ring Meighan (his wife), George Sims, Mrs. George Sims (Marjorie Bartlett Byington), Earl Benham, Mrs. Earl Benham, Jimmie Benham (the nine-year-old son of Earl and Christine), Mrs. Raymond Hitchcock (the actor professionally known as Flora Zabelle, the wife of actor Raymond Hitchcock and the sister of Christine Mangasarian), George Holland (a New York reporter who became the publisher of the *New Port Richey Press*) and Mrs. James Meighan (Meighan's sister-in-law).

So, what links the Meighans, the Simses, the Hitchcocks and the Benhams to New Port Richey? Most likely, Meighan visited the city at the recommendation of members of his elite social network in Great Neck, Long Island, and its Kings Village and Kings Point. Thomas and Frances

Thomas Meighan speaks at Sims Park during the dedication of the Main Street Bridge over the Cotee River, 1927. *West Pasco Historical Society.*

Meighan owned an estate on Grenwolde Drive in Great Neck. George and Marjorie Sims owned an estate in Great Neck. Entertainment professionals Raymond Hitchocock and Flora Zabelle owned an estate on Sunset Drive in Kings Point, facing the Long Island Sound. The Benhams owned an estate across the sound in Connecticut.

For one brief, shining moment, these couples danced under the wrought iron chandeliers of the Hacienda Hotel.

7

THE THOMAS MEIGHAN THEATRE

Many erroneously believe motion picture actor Thomas Meighan built the cinema named in his honor on the northwest corner of Grand Boulevard and Nebraska Avenue. However, The Meighan Theatre was named in tribute to the famous star who adopted New Port Richey as his favorite Florida city and who was instrumental in attracting to it some of the brightest stars of the stage and screen.

On March 13, 1925, *New Port Richey Press* reported that John S. Jackson, the owner of the Palms Theatre on Main Street, expected to begin construction within ninety days on a new forty-by-one-hundred-foot theater on Main Street west of the current location and that the old building would be razed. However, plans for a new Palms Theatre never materialized. Instead, Jackson became the manager of the Meighan Theatre, and he and the town's citizenry hoped Meighan would be on hand to crack a bottle of champagne over the cornerstone of the theater for its grand opening.

On September 4, 1925, *New Port Richey Press* reported:

$50,000 MOVIE HOUSE TO BE BUILT SOON

A new $50,000 motion picture theatre will be built on the [northwest] *corner Filling Station, according to an announcement just made by the incorporators of the Richey Amusement Company, which is now in process of formation, with a fully paid up capital of $50,000. The incorporators of the new company are W.K. Jahn, James W. Clark, E.A. Leeston-*

Smith, Charles. W. Barnett, F.I. Grey, and F.E. Dingus. Officers of the company will be Jas. W. Clark, president; E.A. Leeston-Smith and F.L. Grey, vice-president; W.K. Jahn, secretary and Chas. W. Barnett, assistant secretary and treasurer.

The site of the new theatre was purchased from E.A. Leeston-Smith and is one of the corners of his valuable block recently purchased from M.C. Brake. The building will be 50 by 95 feet, of modified Moorish type, of stucco finish in colors. The front and side of the building will be of ornate design and handsome of appearance according to a sketch which has already been received from the architect. Plans for the building are now being prepared and construction will start within thirty days.

The theatre has been leased to Calkins & Hudson, of Brooksville, who will operate it. The theatre will be equipped with opera seats and will have a capacity of 500, including a gallery seating about 150. Plans also provide for a suitable stage with drop curtains and other equipment for vaudeville and plays.

On June 25, 1926, as the theater's grand opening loomed, the *New Port Richey Press* announced:

New Port Richey's beautiful new motion picture theatre has been named the "Thomas Meighan Theatre" in tribute to the famous film star who has adopted New Port Richey as his favorite Florida city and who has been largely instrumental in interesting here some of the brightest stars of the screen and stage....It was hoped that Mr. Meighan would be on hand to crack a bottle of champagne over the corner-stone of the theatre. It was found to be impossible for the famous screen star to be present in person, but the next best happening is announced with the statement that the picture house's first attraction will be Thomas Meighan in The New Klondike, *a picture of Florida during the boom.*

Naming the theater after a national celebrity—who had purchased land in the city, planned the construction of a winter home and invited his illustrious northern colleagues—served as an effective marketing strategy by Richey Amusement Company. Now, the theater would host the premieres of films produced by Famous Players–Lasky, the employer of the city's resident motion picture star and his studio colleagues. Leased to an operating company, the theater ensured "high class pictures and entertainment."

The article also named the theater's architect, Thomas Reed Martin from Chicago, who had relocated to Florida and designed residences and public spaces in Sarasota and Tampa. Martin would later design Thomas Meighan's New Port Richey estate, the Pasco building, several riverside mansions and the Hacienda Hotel.

In an article in the *New Port Richey Press* from October 23, 1925, under the headline, "Handsome New Theatre to Be Erected: Work Starts Next Week on New Theatre," readers learned of the groundbreaking and saw Martin's original rendering of the elevation of the show palace. With the architect's signature visible in the lower right-hand corner, the published image was more elaborate than the final design. Martin originally designed a three-story building with a Moorish "keyhole" entry arch, reminiscent of the Tampa Bay Hotel (now the University of Tampa), flanked by two domed turrets at each end.

Eventually, the theater was reduced to two stories with the illusion of a third-story balcony with triple arcading arches and column piers over its grand lobby's entrance. Three receding arches resting on three twisted columns on each side replaced the original design's Moorish "keyhole" entry. The domed turrets on each side of the building were replaced with a center dome over the lobby.

On July 1, 1926, the Meighan Theatre appropriately opened to a capacity audience with a screening of *The New Klondike*, starring Thomas Meighan, a romantic comedy written by Ring Lardner set against the backdrop of the Florida land boom speculation and filmed in Miami. The plot involved a small-town pitcher, Thomas Kelly (Thomas Meighan), participating in spring training with a minor-league baseball team in Florida. After being fired by the team's jealous manager, Kelly is then recruited as the celebrity endorser for a Florida real estate firm, and he successfully facilitates his former teammates investing in the firm. Jealous of Kelly's popularity, the manager conspires with a crooked broker to sell Kelly and the investors worthless swampland. Kelly and his friends lose their investment, but Kelly labors to recoup their losses. Eventually, Kelly earns a fortune, repays the investors and is appointed team manager. In this film, did life imitate art, or did art imitate life?

According to the *New Port Richey Press*, more than one hundred disappointed individuals were unable to obtain one of the five hundred seats for the $60,000 theater's grand opening, and J.S. Jackson announced the installation of a complete cooling system in the new playhouse. Although Meighan did not attend the opening, he sent one of the many congratulatory telegrams

The Thomas Meighan Theatre, designed by Thomas Reed Martin, opened with a screening of Meighan's latest film, *The New Klondike*, on July 1, 1926. *West Pasco Historical Society.*

read from the stage by Charles DeWoody (who later spoke at the opening of the Hacienda Hotel) and State Senator Jesse M. Mitchell from Elfers. Mitchell was elected from the Ninth District and served from 1923 to 1927 and again from 1927 to 1931.

"Allow me to congratulate you on the beautiful new theater named Thomas Meighan," read the wire representing Florida governor John W. Martin, "which I feel sure will afford wonderful entertainment for the people of your vicinity."

Telegrams also arrived from John Wellborn Martin, the twenty-fourth governor of Florida from 1925 to 1929; Adolph Zukor, a film producer and cofounder of Paramount Pictures; Sidney R. Kent, a distribution manager of Famous Players–Lasky (later known as Paramount Pictures), president of Fox Studios and cocreator of 20th Century Fox Studios; Ed Wynn, a radio and film actor; Gene Buck, a musical theater lyricist and author of numerous Ziegfeld Follies; David Warfield, a stage actor; Earl Benham, a stage actor, composer, costumer and tailor; and local developers George R. Sims, Warren E. Burns and James H. Becker.

"Permit me to express the deep gratification you have given me by calling your new theater Thomas Meighan," the namesake actor's telegram read. "Thank you for the great compliment, and may you have a fine opening and ever-increasing success."

"On behalf of the Famous Players–Lasky Corporation, allow me to wish you the greatest success in the new operation of your new Thomas Meighan Theatre," Zukor's telegram began. "We feel it a great honor that you saw fit to name your new theater after one of our stars. Depend on us to give you every cooperation."

"Congratulations on the opening of your new theatre," wrote comedian Ed Wynn, Meighan's next-door neighbor in Great Neck. "With a booster like George R. Sims, with a newspaper like George Holland has given you, with a theatre the name of which is already known all over the world, it seems to me you folks are pretty lucky. Now, if you only get an Ed Wynn Park, you will find people will be asking how far New York is from New Port Richey instead of asking as they do now how far New Port Richey is from New York." A roar of laughter and applause rose above the auditorium.

"The opening of the new Thomas Meighan Theatre marks a long forward step in the progress of New Port Richey," read the telegram from George R. Sims. "Few cities the size of ours can boast such a beautiful playhouse. Congratulations to the men whose foresight and enterprise made this possible."

The stock market crash of 1929 occurred on October 24, when share prices on the New York Stock Exchange collapsed. They reached their lowest point on October 29, known as Black Tuesday, when the Dow Jones

The Thomas Meighan Theatre and Leeston-Smith building, circa 1926. *West Pasco Historical Society*.

Industrial Average dropped by 30.57 percent. Triggered by a speculative bubble that burst due to low interest rates, overproduction and excessive credit, the crash led to the worst economic crisis in U.S. history.

The economic climate forced the Meighan Theatre to reduce its admission prices to thirty-five cents for adults and ten cents for children, effective February 7, 1930. Motion pictures played seven days a week; each feature was shown for two nights except for the Saturday feature. The Thomas Meighan Theatre needed its namesake hero to promote business.

On January 16, 1930, Meighan appeared at the theater between the two showings of his silent film *The Racket* (1928), which was nominated for the Academy Award for Best Picture, garnering the theater's largest audience to date. "Promptly at the beginning of the second show," reported the *New Port Richey Press*, "the expectancy of the packed auditorium was rewarded, for Thomas Meighan, in person, left his waiting limousine with Mrs. Meighan and another distinguished looking young lady, and entered the theater. Resounding cheers greeted the famous visitor following his introduction by Warren E. Burns, neighbor of the Meighans at Jasmin Point Estates, voicing appreciation of the entire city and surrounding country at being honored by the presence of the great actor."

The "distinguished" young lady, stage and screen actor Madeline Cameron, had been spending the winter in New Port Richey as a guest of the Meighans. After launching her career in the Metropolitan Opera Ballet, Cameron transitioned to vaudeville and appeared in several Ziegfeld Follies before starring in the Broadway musical *Hit the Deck*. At the time of her visit, Cameron had starred on screen in *The 20th Amendment* (1930), a futuristic musical comedy set in the year 1950 costarring Jack Haley, who is best remembered as the Tin Man in *The Wizard of Oz* (1939).

Meighan Heralds Sound Films in New Port Richey

"Wait a minute, wait a minute," said Al Jolson in *The Jazz Singer* (1927) as the first line of dialogue heard in the first feature-length, part-sound— or part-talking—film. "You ain't heard nothin' yet." The trailblazing film contains barely two minutes of synchronized dialogue and eleven musical numbers. The following year, Warner Brothers introduced the first all-talking feature film, *Lights of New York*, and the gradual transition from silent to sound films commenced.

Sound films reached New Port Richey on Sunday evening, March 9, 1930, when, according to John W. Parkes (publisher of the *New Port Richey Press* from 1926 to 1930), Thomas Meighan pushed the button that premiered sound films at the Meighan Theatre. Leiland Poole had taken over the theater after the start of the Great Depression, an era when few small businesses expanded, and engaged E.B. Kinard of the Audiphone Corporation of America to direct the installation of sound equipment.

Sometime around 1934, falling victim to the Great Depression, the Meighan Theatre closed. However, it soon reopened under a litany of operators and names, serving generations in New Port Richey until 1968.

In 1972, Suncoast Young People's Theater purchased the building, transforming it into a stage playhouse for community theater groups. Renamed the Richey Suncoast Theatre, for over five decades, the venue has entertained generations with quality live entertainment.

Casa Francesca: Thomas Meighan's Estate

"A syndicate of famous folk of the stage and screen has purchased a tract of land here," the *Dade City Banner* reported on March 3, 1926. "The syndicate is composed of Thomas Meighan, Gloria Swanson [legendary film actor], Leon Erroll [film comedian], George Fawcett [stage and film actor], Charlotte Greenwood [film actor and dancer], Dennis F. McSweeney, Victor Heerman [film director and Oscar winner for *Little Women* (1933)], Blanche Ring [actor and Frances Ring Meighan's sister], Charles Winningren [stage and film actor], and Nathan Burkan [copyright lawyer and co-founder of the American Society of Composers]."

"Thomas Meighan concludes purchase of a large tract of land at New Port Richey," the *Dade City Banner* reported nine days later. "Mr. Meighan ordered plans drawn for a house for himself and wife. It is expected all will have homes built on this tract. [Edgar] Selwyn and Sam H. Harris had formerly bought lots in New Port Richey and are planning homes in Pasco County's Gulf City." Selwyn was an actor, playwright, director and producer on Broadway who founded a theatrical production company and owned several Selwyn Theatres. As a New York theater producer and theater owner, Harris partnered with George M. Cohan to produce eighteen Broadway musicals.

Meighan purchased the land from Warren E. Burns of the Burns-Becker Corporation. In 1918, Burns purchased the forty acres with half a mile of west bank river footage as a site for his grapefruit grove, and in 1926, he subdivided the grove into the Jasmin Point Estates for residential development. Each lot offered an unobstructed view of the river. Adjoining the exclusive community, the Jasmin Point Golf Club was under development, its course extending from the river to the gulf.

On April 15, 1927, the *New Port Richey Press* ran the headline "Tom Meighan to Build $40,000 Home at Jasmin Point This November." The article reported Meighan considered New Port Richey his home and intended to vote there. It also said he hoped to make motion pictures in the city.

Jesse L. Lasky (1880–1958). *PICRYL public domain archive, Get Archive LLC (public domain).*

According to Reginald Sims Jr., the Meighans became so absorbed in the construction of their new home that the actor was weeks overdue in Hollywood, where he was under contract to make a series of western movies. Reportedly, a Paramount Pictures producer telephoned the actor daily and flooded him with telegrams, urging him to report to the studio, but to no avail.

Desperate to manage his leading man, the producer—possibly studio executive Jesse L. Lasky—traveled by train to Los Angeles and taxied to New Port Richey from Tarpon Springs. "But Meighan said he wouldn't leave until his home was finished," Sims Jr. recalled. "Finally, in desperation, the producer asked Meighan how much the home was costing him. Meighan replied the cost was $125,000." According to the *New Port Richey Press* in 1927, the estate's original estimated cost was $40,000.

Reportedly, the producer bargained with Meighan: if the actor would return to Los Angeles with the producer, Paramount Pictures would expense the cost of the home. "Meighan got the home as a bonus, and it didn't cost him a cent," reported Sims Jr. "I happen to know that this really happened."

Completed in 1928, Casa Francesca, named after Frances Meighan, lay on 4.15 acres with 683 feet of river frontage, access to the gulf only 2 miles away and 641 feet of road frontage. Reached through a formal gate, the walled mansion was set back 180 feet from the road and accessed through an entrance drive and circle. The thirteen-room residence contained four master bedrooms, four and a half baths, three bedrooms and three baths

Casa Francesca, the Meighan Estate at Jasmin Point, designed by Thomas Reed Martin. *West Pasco Historical Society.*

for servants. Enhanced by a red tile roof, patios, porches and balconies, Casa Francesca featured high, beamed ceilings, spacious rooms, casement windows and French doors facing the river. It also had a sunken living room and sunroom and floors of polished oak and Spanish tile. The bedrooms offered walk-in closets and built-in conveniences. An unusually large, 60-by-33-foot tiled swimming pool with patio and cabana changing spaces overlooked an adjacent 3-acre citrus grove with grapefruit, orange, lemon and tangelo plants. An attached two-car garage contained a chauffeur's quarters and utility room with laundry appliances. The property was further insulated by a riverfront park separated by a fence and bamboo.

See chapter 17 to learn the fate of Thomas Meighan's Casa Francesca.

8

A COMMUNITY HOTEL

In George Sims's *Revised Plan for the Town of New Port Richey*, published in a brochure in 1915, block B on Riverside Place was noted as being "reserved for hotel." Eleven years later, the hotel came to fruition, but it was far grander than its original concept, thanks to the prominent figures who flocked to the city for the winter season. This hotel's luxury accommodations, more elaborate than those at the Sass Hotel or Hotel Newport, met the standards of silent screen actor Thomas Meighan.

On New Year's Eve 1925, the *Tampa Bay Times* reported: "An operating company comprising businessmen of New Port Richey, Miami, Boston, and New York have deposited earnest money on a site chosen for a combined hotel and country club which it is expected will be under construction within sixty days. The new hotel, according to present designs, will have rooms with baths for 100 guests, and will be known as 'The Hacienda.' The architecture will be of Morocco-type. It will be designed in wings, with a spacious terrace in the center."

On March 5, 1926, the *New Port Richey Press* announced the local Civitan Club had launched a campaign to raise $100,000 for a $250,000 hotel and published a letter from James E. Meighan (Thomas Meighan's brother) to Edgar A. Wright, chairman of the hotel committee, dated March 4, 1926. The letter read:

James E. Meighan's generous offer of land to build the Hacienda Hotel makes headlines in the *New Port Richey Press*, March 5, 1926. *West Pasco Historical Society*.

Dear Mr. Mayor:

Understanding that the city of New Port Richey is desirous of building a hotel, I wish to offer absolutely free and clear, lots one, two, three, eleven, twelve, thirteen, fourteen, fifteen…and…sixteen, Block three of Port Richey Company's sub-division to New Port Richey—same facing one hundred and fifty feet on Main street, running back two hundred and thirty feet on Riverside Place [today's Bank Street]*—and having a frontage of one hundred and fifty feet on Sims Park.*

This offer is unrestricted, the only condition being that a hotel consisting of not less than sixty (60) rooms exclusive of apartments be erected according to plans acceptable to your hotel committee and starting not less than six (6) months from date.

This proposition will remain open for thirty (30) days.

Very truly yours,
James E. Meighan

On March 19, 1926, the *New Port Richey Press* reported:

The drive for $100,000 to [ensure] *construction of New Port Richey's quarter of a million dollar hotel, to be erected on a site donated by James E. Meighan, on Main street, was two-thirds completed last night, when a summation of the subscriptions showed that more than $64,000 had been signed for in four days.*

It is predicted that the drive will have been successfully consummated within a week, and that building plans will be entered into at once. The fact that New Port Richey realizes the need of a hotel such as the one contemplated has been clearly exemplified in the total of the subscriptions thus far, despite the stringency of the local money market.

There is still the necessity of raising more than $35,000, to make the total count $100,000 but scores of prospects (persons with the interest of New Port Richey at heart) are yet to be heard from.

Unofficial tabulations from drive headquarters in the chamber of commerce building show that one hundred and nine persons have subscribed for the hotel stock, and that only four subscriptions for amounts as great as $5,000 have been received.

An energetic committee of drive workers, headed by Walter K. Jahn and under the personal direction of Dr. Hunt and Charles Snell will continue to ply their public-spirited trade of solicitation until the necessary amount is raised.

New Port Richey in West Coast Baseball Loop

NEW PORT RICHEY PRESS

A Weekly Paper for the West Coast of Pasco County

VOLUME 9.—No. 11.   NEW PORT RICHEY, FLORIDA, FRIDAY, MARCH 12, 1926. $2.00 Per Annum In Advance

NEW HOTEL PLANS READY

City is Bubbling With Enthusiasm

MAGNIFICENT STRUCTURE WILL NOT COST LESS THAN QUARTER OF MILLION; ARCHITECT MARTIN COMPLETES DRAWINGS

By JOHN CLEVE CULBERTSON
(Peerless Continental Commentator on Florida Facts and Fancies)

THE FACTS FIRST!
THE FANCIES LATER!

The first fact first. New Port Richey will have within six months a marvellous hotel. On that fact I am going to dwell to the extent of repetition. New Port Richey will have within six months a marvellous hotel. New Port Richey is going to have a beauty of a hotel. The city is going to have a hotel which dreamers have created, a structure of beauty which has sprung from the brain of a genius-architect named Martin, an architect indigenous to this part of Florida, but whose name and fame, I predict will spread throughout the land, to Mars, yea, to the Moon and beyond! He is a master! His pencil-point has devised a master's creation. The creation is the master-hotel which in the minds of the city's nobles already is limned, graceful and inspiring, as it will appear in actuality when it is completed a scant six months hence.

And when this beauty-hotel rears its magnificence above the present sky-line of a mavellous little community, recall the words of your veracious correspondent. He, in case you do not know is acting not as "a prophet in his own home town". He is a visitor. He assures you that he knows! He is in your midst for the occasion and but newly. He is here in New Port Richey at the behest of the irrepressible and young Mr. Holland,—here to employ the shooting irons of the newspaper gentry to see, that the city's most important current need is a need no more.

So, once again, and finally, New Port Richey is going to have a modern, artistic hotel, to be erected at a probable cost of $250,000 and to be subscribed by the most far-seeing of the many fore-sighted men and women of brains in as live a miniature municipality as there is in the world today.

One can approach the subject of New Port Richey's new hotel with a jaunty air. Your city inspires jauntiness. It has a swank about it which is individual. It's the top hat of the cities in this blue-chip area. Watch it go. A professional observer, a skeptic too, says it must. You watch it.

It was the writer's pleasure last night, his presence unknown, to attend the Civitan Club meeting at the Enchanting Inn. Hardly a Crillon, your Enchanting Inn, nor a Ruhl, but a good comfortable place for all of that, and peopled by an extraordinary, intelligent, earnest and ambitious group of citizens.

I, fresh from the social demands of the east coast strand, and barely recovered, (the word is used advisedly) from a session at the Riviera, found the occasion invigorating. One's waistcoat was in no manner a curiosity. Intentness, a common cause, good-fellowship, the birth of a new and greater city, those were the issues.

I listened with severe interest to the proceedings. A gentleman named De Forrest was in palbable charge of events. The man's caliber insured the success of any thing over which he presides. He has done, I say upon most cursory observance of his demeanor great things. I, of whom if one were present of the work of committees, recently appointed I am told, and of the general zealous response to initial overture on the subject of providing your city with a great, new hotel, a feature which will be the making of you all,—if I do not presume.

You will be interested to know what has been done through the week. A committee of Civitans, a sub-committee of a general drive committee of fifteen, entrusted to the club with comprehensive plans for chartering a corporation to finance the hotel.
(Continued on Page Five).

Randall Offers His Water-Works To City

COUNCIL NAMES COMMITTEE TO CONSIDER PURCHASE

One of the most important items brought before the city council at its meeting last Tuesday evening was the offer for sale to the city, by E. L. Randall, of the city water works for $15,000.

Upon the presentation, by council president Shaw of this offer, Councilman Max Goodman, strenuously objected, saying he would not go on record as having been a party to a vote on a proposition that had been refused by referendum.

Councilman Haw concurred with Dr. Goodman, whereupon Councilman
(Continued on Page Eight).

Mayor Wright In Official Attire At Governor's Ball

IN COMPLETE REGALIA as a Colonel of the Governor's staff, Mayor Edgar A. Wright of New Port Richey was snapped at the Governor's Ball as one of a group of the state's executive's closest friends and advisors. This unique feature of the picture is printed today to let our thousands of readers know that the best little ol' Mayor in the whole Sunshine State is appreciated by others as well as by ourselves.

CITY BALL CLUB IN LEAGUE

By FRED FRIERSON

Representatives were here yesterday from Clearwater, Dade City, and New Port Richey, and meeting in the offices of the West Coast Base Ball league.

The league is to be a four-team circuit, the above-mentioned cities, with the addition of Plant City, forming the loop.

The delegates from the various towns agreed unanimously on the fundamental issues and organized along the following lines:

1—The season will open April
(Continued on Page Five).

Noted War Nurse, 86 Years Young, Visits Town

MRS. GERMAINE, "VET" OF CIVIL WAR BUYS IN CITY

By GEO. H. GRIST

Mrs. Linda Germaine, of Detroit, America's most famous nurse, is in New Port Richey as the guest of Mr. and Mrs. Paul Custer.

Mrs. Germaine ,who is eighty-six, but who hopes to live long enough to look her age, has the honor of being the first graduate nurse in America.

So much account had she in her profession that Mrs. Germane, became the Florence Nightingale of the 10th Michigan Infantry ,when these boys fought through the civil war. However, blue and gray looked alike to her, for her cause was humanity, and under her care came many of the men of both sides.

After the war Mrs. Germane still carried on her duties as a nurse, but her carreer was to associate itself with another war, the Spanish-American, in which she did valiant work with the American soldiers, and again at its early culmination took up her duties as a professional nurse.

Among her most famous patients was John D. Rockefeller, whom she treated at the Battle Creek sanitarium. During a talk with the famous "oil king", John D. Rockefeller suggested to Mrs. Germane that he would give her a million dollars for a new stomach. "Go to Florida", suggested our famous nurse, and to Florida
(Continued on Page Eight).

Water Carnival to Be Held On Friday Next

GALA DAY PLANNED BY NINNEMAN FOR MAR. 19TH

By PAT O'DEA

The most ambitious water carnival ever attempted in New Port Richey is planned for next Friday, coincident with the sale by auction of River Gulf Point, a tract of land at the Millionaire's Row, where the Cotee River flows into the Gulf of Mexico.

N. P. Ninneman, the auctioneer, is sponsoring the water show and has offered an assortment of valuable prizes to winners of various events scheduled for that day.

Chief among the features is to a handicap boat race, for power boats of not more than twenty-five horse power. Another feature is to be a sprint and distance swimming race, to be contested by residents of New Port Richey, Tarpon Springs, Elfers and Dade City. Another event will be a canting contest from the sea-wall of River Gulf Point, in which local fishermen are urged to participate. The prizes to be offered are said to be well worthy the serious attention of any sportsman in the vicinity.

Entries of any of these events should be made in writing to N. P. Ninnemann or any member of this staff. The auctioneer's organization will be busy this week in the city, making preparations for the sale. In addition to the water sports, a free Ford car and prizes of cash and household effects are to be given away to attendants at the sale.
(Continued on Page Eight).

CITY CLERK IS IMPROVING.

W. A. Lockard, city clerk of New Port Richey, has been confined to a sick-bed, during the past week owing to a serious infection of the face, caused by an infected molar.

Mr. Lockard, who has been reported as very low, is now on the road to a complete recovery, and it is likely will be seen at his desk in the city hall, within the next week or two.

New Port Richey Press announces the city's "bubbling enthusiasm" for architect Thomas Reed Martin's design for the Hacienda Hotel, March 12, 1926. *West Pasco Historical Society.*

New Port Richey Press encourages the community's investment in the Hacienda Hotel and publishes Thomas Reed Martin's original elevation of the structure and gardens on March 15, 1926. *West Pasco Historical Society*.

By April 9, New Port Richey's enthusiastic citizens raised $72,000 for the sixty-room hotel, paid in cash through stock subscriptions led by Charles DeWoody. The public followed each advance in the hotel's construction with avid interest, and the city perceived it as the most important item of news affecting its destiny. Commonly referred to as the Community Hotel Project, its rapid progress signified the modern development of New Port Richey, which had been a rustic pioneer town only a decade before.

New Port Richey's citizenry who had settled over the previous fourteen years and those in neighboring areas—Elfers, Seven Springs and Tarpon Springs—whose parents and grandparents had been pioneers soon commingled with affluent northern transplants, a pattern that continued over the next century. This melding of common folk and the elite became

Two-thirds of the funds needed to build the Hacienda Hotel are raised in the first four days of a drive. *Published in* New Port Richey Press, *March 19, 1926; West Pasco Historical Society.*

an interesting juxtaposition. This was no better exemplified than during the Florida boom of 1926, when Mediterranean Revival mansions sprang up along the riverfront across from modest Craftsman bungalows.

On April 19, the *New Port Richey Press* published Thomas Reed Martin's color renderings of two mansions in the Mediterranean Revival style for Warren E. Burns and James H. Becker. "The residences are to be built this summer by the partners of the Burns-Becker Realty Co., owners and developers of Jasmin Point," announced the newspaper, "and will greatly add the prestige of New Port Richey as a residential resort."

With a plan to elevate the city for affluent investors, both men and other involved parties needed a luxury hotel to serve as the town's cultural and social center and turned to Martin for its design. Martin had designed the Thomas Meighan Theatre and the Pasco building, both completed

With adequate funds raised, the Hacienda Hotel will become a reality. *Published in* New Port Richey Press, *March 26, 1926; West Pasco Historical Society.*

in 1926. Thomas Meighan had also commissioned Martin to design his residence on the Pithlachascotee River, completed in 1928.

On June 4, 1926, the board of directors of the Community Hotel formally accepted plans submitted by Thomas Reed Martin for the interior and exterior of the structure. The modern fifty-room hotel would be built at a cost not to exceed $100,000 in "extreme Spanish design," equipped with a steam-heating plant and comfortably furnished throughout. Martin included a large courtyard, north- and south-facing open verandas, an open-air dining room surrounded by palms and a spacious dining room and lobby adorned with Spanish-beamed ceilings and ornate plaster corbels and wrought iron chandeliers. The chamber of commerce displayed the architect's renderings of the lobby and main dining room for public viewing. Crowds gathered to study the design, delighting in the prospect of the hotel putting New Port Richey on the map.

Two weeks later, a crew broke ground on the densely foliaged site—with stunning views of Enchantment Park, the Pithlachascotee River and Orange

Lake—and cleared trees and shrubs in the footprint of the structure. As the landscaping design involved only a small portion of the trees on site, uprooted palms were made available for public consumption.

By June 18, 1926, directors of the hotel committee had formally approved the hotel's plans and specifications and invited prospective contractors who wished to bid on the hotel's construction to contact the chamber of commerce to obtain copies of the specifications. The directors projected the hotel's completion by December 15, an opening ball on New Year's Eve 1926 and readiness for occupancy by January 15, 1927.

W. Barnett of the First State Bank received monthly payments from stockholders, and although the committee welcomed additional stock subscriptions to raise a sum of at least $100,000, directors announced assurance of the financial end of the project.

The city council considered passing general and assessment bonds of more than $500,000, sufficient to "lift the town out of the bushes" and into a new "league" to meet the standards of its affluent new residents and visitors. General bonds of $100,000 would provide for the beautification of the city's park system, paving of the Circle, erection of a city hall and public library and construction of an athletic field. Assessment bonds of $400,000 levied against property owners would fund the paving and guttering of the sidewalks of important streets in the city's incorporated limits.

In preparation for the hotel and its guests, the city paved Main Street to the river, and Riverside Drive (today's Bank Street) afforded a new paved entrance to the hotel. The city's complexion improved with the resurfacing of these two streets, along with the installation of fourteen streetlights to illuminate the streets leading to the hotel site.

The *New Port Richey Press* rallied citizens to support efforts to fund improvements. "You, as a citizen of New Port Richey, or as an interested property owner should do not less than demand the immediate passage of the proposed special and general bonds," the newspaper commended. In bold capital letters, the local press urged, "THOSE BONDS MUST PASS." Pressure mounted.

On August 9, 1925, the *St. Petersburg Times* reported:

> *Plans have been set on foot at an enthusiastic meeting of New Port Richeyites for the construction of a 100-room fire-proof hotel. Within a few minutes after the meeting was called to order, nearly the entire capital required was subscribed.*

The site selected is a tract overlooking the beautiful Pithlachascotee River, north of the Gulf high school building and in the exact center of population. The site has the further advantage of being located within a short distance of the proposed station of the West Coast railway, now an assured fact.

The structure will be of the most modern construction and will be either of Moorish or Spanish type. There will be in the first unit 55 rooms, elegantly appointed, and each room equipped with a private bath. The hotel grounds will overlook the river for more than 300 feet and are well shaded with palms and other semi-tropical forest growth and shrubbery.

The estimated cost is $150,000 and the structure will be ready for opening before the beginning of January.

By July 2, the hotel corporation had raised $82,000 through stock subscriptions, led by Charles F. DeWoody. The corporation had also sped up its plans to ensure an opening by the end of the year. In response to the $18,000 balance, Warren E. Burns and James H. Becker, who had already invested heavily in the project, guaranteed their underwriting of the hotel's financing for up to an additional $25,000. With the hotel's completion in reach, DeWoody resigned as president and suggested the electron of Burns, given his large financial contribution.

James Meighan led the charge for the hotel's construction by donating the land, valued at $50,000, and was joined by local men, including George R. Sims, the father of New Port Richey. Officers of the hotel corporation, officially known as Community Hotel Inc., were Warren E. Burns, president; James E. Meighan, vice-president; James H. Becker, vice-president and treasurer; and Charles F. Hoffman, secretary. The corporation's directors were Warren E. Burns, James H. Becker, Edward C. Blum, C.W. Barnett, Edward P. Campbell, Charles F. DeWoody, Frank I. Grey, Charles F. Hoffman, Dr. William W. Hunt, Moses A. Fullington, James E. Meighan, Richard Morgan, Leland C. Poole, Fred A. Shaw, George R. Sims, Charles E. Snell and Edgar A. Wright.

By August 27, 1926, The Hacienda's foundation was under construction with a crew digging trenches. Superintendent Oliver Le May expected the first-floor joists to be laid the following week and a significant amount of flooring installed to justify a "progress celebration," and plans were discussed to host an open-air dance on site on the hotel's first floor. Gulf Utilities Company of New Port Richey wired the hotel and furnished electrical fixtures, and Cason and McSwaine, mason contractors from Brooksville, provided stuccoing and plastering services. F.W. Hill Plumbing Company of Tarpon Springs rounded out the list of contractors.

At a weekly Civitan's Dinner in September 1926, Warren E. Burns updated the group on the progress of the Community Hotel. In response to the rumor that those building the hotel had come from other towns, Burns asserted out-of-town workmen were hired only after local men had been given adequate opportunity to bid on the work. He also introduced William H. Loveland, who praised contractor Oliver Le May's ability to deliver the hotel "finished well and economically." Loveland humorously disclosed having under his clothing a severe sunburn that would serve upon his return to New York as a beautiful memento of his visit to New Port Richey.

Through their vision and industry, Warren E. Burns and James H. Becker were directly responsible for The Hacienda.

9

NEW PORT RICHEY'S ELITE

The Men Who Built the Hacienda Hotel

WHO WERE THE PRESIDENT AND VICE-PRESIDENT OF COMMUNITY HOTEL INC.?

Warren E. Burns (1876–1941), a prominent developer in New Port Richey in the 1920s, was president of the Burns-Becker Realty Company, which built the Hacienda Hotel, and president of Burns Florida Corporation, a citrus brokerage firm. Burns was the largest property owner in New Port Richey outside the Port Richey Company and held controlling interest in the Gulf Utilities Company, which provided electric power in the city. In partnership with James H. Becker in a realty business, Burns developed the exclusive Jasmin Point and Old Grove subdivisions. In 1928, Burns served as the acting mayor of New Port Richey.

Born in Milford Junction, Indiana, Burns relocated to New York in 1909, before Florida beckoned him and wife, Lola L. Burns. Burns was a member of the Pear of the West Masonic Lodge in New Port Richey and the Egypt Temple Shrine in Tampa. In January 1941, he underwent surgery in Tampa and

PORT RICHEY PRESS FRIDAY, MARCH 4 1927

Partners in New Port Richey's Making

THE BURNS-BECKER CORPORATION. Owners and developers of Jasmin Point and Old Grove, owners of the Gulf Utilities Company and the West Florida Bond and Mortgage Company, financers of The Hacienda and active leaders in every movement tending toward the high-class development of this city, Warren E. Burns (left) and James H. Becker (right) are the prime movers today in New Port Richey's marvellous growth. Men of wealth and integrity, their word is indeed accepted as their bond, and the fame of the city is growing apace with their good works for its success.

Warren E. Burns and James H. Becker, local developers and the main financiers of the Hacienda Hotel, pose in front of the hotel. *Published in* New Port Richey Press, *March 4, 1927; West Pasco Historical Society.*

anticipated a second surgery. Burns died several weeks later, on February 7, in a Tampa hospital.

James H. Becker (1864–1931), Burns's partner in the Burns-Becker Corporation, arrived in New Port Richey in 1926 from Ohio, where his family owned the Elmore Manufacturing Company, which produced bicycles and automobiles until it was sold to General Motors in 1910. Burns served as chairman of the First State Bank of New Port Richey. Becker's wife, Metta Angell Becker (1860–1931), died suddenly on New Year's Day 1931, and he died in his mansion in Jamine Point forty-three days later.

"We advertise no buy we would not make ourselves," Burns-Becker's advertisements announced in the *New Port Richey Press* during the boom of the 1920s. "A purchase advised by us is never a gamble but an investment."

Burns and Becker co-owned and developed Jasmin Point and the Old Grove, choosing to build their own winter homes in exclusive Jasmin Point. Their vision for New Port Richey dovetailed with those of another Tampa Bay developer.

The Predictions of Burks L. Hamner

In August 1926, Burks L. Hamner, a Tampa real estate developer—one of Florida's visionaries and the largest empire builder in South Florida—and his associates addressed New Port Richey's Civitan Club with his predictions for the development of Tampa and its neighboring communities and its impact on New Port Richey.

Hamner had attained success when he partnered with several other investors to create Tampa's Temple Terrace and had been credited with establishing the Parkland Estates neighborhood just west of Howard Avenue between Swann and Morrison Avenues.

Hamner envisioned the terminus of one long Main Street, which he described as "a prosperous district inhabited by more than two millions of persons." The main street would include New Port Richey's Grand Boulevard, which Hamner explained, "has caused [the city] to be acclaimed as one of the four beauty spots of the state." The artery would continue through Elfers, Tarpon Springs, Palm Harbor, Ozona, Safety Harbor, Dunedin, Clearwater, Bellaire, Largo, Tampa Shores, Tampa, St. Petersburg, Pinellas Park, Bradenton, Manatee, Palmetto and Sarasota. In less than ten years,

Hamner predicted, a visitor to the area's densely populated main artery would be unable to differentiate each city's boundaries.

Long before President Dwight D. Eisenhower's Interstate Highway System (created by the Federal Aid Highway Act of 1956), which later produced Interstate 275, Hammer arguably introduced a concept that eventually came to fruition, although deviating from his proposed path: U.S. Highway 19.

"I have a very distinct recollection of addressing you about six years ago when Tampa had the population of about 50,000 people," Hamner continued, "and at that time I told you that Tampa would have about 200,000 people on or before the year 1930. Many thought I was crazy. The kindest among you said I was an optimist. It is not 1930 yet, and we already have 200,000. I say to you that Tampa and its built-up environs will have a population of one million people in 1936." The Great Depression impacted Hamner's prediction; Tampa Bay's population surpassed 1 million by 1970.

While Burks L. Hamner revealed his predictions for the greater Tampa Bay area, the sounds of saws and hammers reverberated through New Port Richey.

MANSIONS RISE ON THE RIVERBANK

While the emergent hotel promised the city notoriety and prosperity, the citizens were abuzz in the spring and summer of 1926, with three mammoth mansions rising in Jasmin Point on the western side of the Pithlachascotee River for affluent and distinguished northerners.

In August 1926, the *New Port Richey Press* reported, "With three magnificent residences fast rising above the ground, with the water system in operation already, with miles of sidewalks, roads, and curbing in place, Jasmin Point, the Burns-Becker development, on the west bank of the river, is looming now as the most beautiful residential tract on the West Coast of Florida."

Instead of using sun-absorbent, glaring white sidewalk paving, Burns-Becker tinted the cement with a reddish hue that was more soothing to the eyes and harmonious with the horticulture design of the neighborhood. Their building materials featured successive blocks of tile containing ventilation apertures worthy of construction in Palm Beach.

The Becker-Moore Estate

James H. Becker's personal residence built in the Mediterranean Revival style at 5525 Bamboo Lane, on the river's west bank, boasted a cement boat deck and ornamental striped awnings on its abundance of windows overlooking the river. Designed by Thomas Reed Martin, Becker's home featured prominently in a 1927 brochure for luxury housing with the title *New Port Richey: The Paradise of Florida*. The brochure's cover contained a view of the river from Becker's rear patio.

Today, locals refer to the city's iconic mansion as the Becker-Moore House, as when James H. Becker died in 1931, Dr. Hugh Kelsea Moore, a noted chemist and author, and his wife, Mary Esther Tebbetts, purchased it as a winter residence. When Dr. Moore died in 1939, ownership of the house passed to his son, Hugh Kelsea Moore II. Later, Dr. Basil M. Moodie (1872–1960) of Tampa purchased the home and subsequently sold it to Charles Fournier, a Canadian resident who spent his winters in New Port Richey. Since 2016, David and Jeanette Lee have owned the historic home, now painted in a flamingo pink.

Architect Thomas Reed Martin designed the Mediterranean Revival residences of William L. Loveland (*left*) and James H. Becker (*right*) at Jasmin Point; both survive. *West Pasco Historical Society*.

According to his obituary in the *Sun-Journal*, Dr. Hugh Kelsea Moore, an internationally known research director for thirty years with the Brown Company of Portland, Maine, died in Dunedin, Florida, following a severe heart attack in his New Port Richey home. Moore was renowned for his research in wood pulp and paper making. Born in Andover, Massachusetts, Moore attended the Massachusetts Institute of Technology and received an honorary degree from the University of Maine.

In 1920, Moore authored numerous scientific books and received the gold medal from the American Institute of Chemical Engineers for "the best contributions to applied science since 1913" and the Perkins Medal in 1925. Also in 1925, Moore served as the president of the American Institute of Chemical Engineers and was a member of the Chemical Engineering Commission.

During World War I, Moore assisted the government through his service in the Council of National Defense and Naval Consulting Board of New Hampshire. He served in the New Hampshire legislature in 1923–24 and was a candidate in the 1929 primaries for the governorship of New Hampshire.

After retiring in 1934 from his position as chief chemist for Brown-Burgess Sulphite Fibre Company, where he operated paper mills in the United States and Canada, Moore, with his wife, became a "snowbird," maintaining a summer residence in York Harbor, Maine, and a winter residence in New Port Richey.

The Burns Estate

Warren E. Burns, the co-owner and codeveloper of Jasmin Point and Old Grove, spent winters in New Port Richey with his wife, Lola. They built a Mediterranean Revival–style mansion designed by Thomas Reed Martin for $85,000 on the west side of the river, near the Beckers. Burns served as the president of the New Port Richey City Council. Burns also maintained a yacht and a captain, frequently sailing on the river and spending days at sea in the gulf. Later, the Burns estate was purchased by S.O. Aungst and Ken and Abby Misemer.

Home of W.E.Burnes
New Port Richey, Fla.

Photo
Palmetto Studio

Above: The estate of Warren E. Burns, designed by Thomas Reed Martin, was razed in 2002. *West Pasco Historical Society.*

Right: *Left to right*: Developer Warren E. Burns; Frank R. Steele, the first manager of the Hacienda Hotel; and Joseph J. Foley, a prominent winter resident, Jasmin Point Golf Course, circa 1930. *West Pasco Historical Society*.

BURNS AND BECKER'S DEVELOPMENT

The Burns-Becker Corporation purchased a full-page advertisement in the December 10, 1926 edition of *New Port Richey Press*, in which it gloated about Florida's mild winter weather while reporting on the hotel's progress:

New York Under a Blanket of Snow

While New York and other northern cities were suffering from severe winds and cold on Sunday last, we of New Port Richey were enjoying outdoor swimming, golfing and fishing. While northern roads are surfaced with ice and slush, what a pleasure it has been to drive through this country at this time, seeing the trees with their heavy burden of oranges, grapefruit, and tangerines.

Have you been keeping your eyes on The Hacienda, the new hotel? The contractors tell us they are right on schedule, the furniture and kitchen equipment have all been ordered, and what a credit it will be, not only to this town but to the entire state.

In New Port Richey, the real estate development boom peaked from 1925 to 1928, and The Hacienda became the epitome of its extravagance.

10

THE HACIENDA'S ARCHITECT

Thomas Reed Martin

The Hacienda Hotel is a prime example of the Mediterranean Revival architectural style defined by the Florida boom of the 1920s. The style reflects the architectural influences of the Mediterranean coast: Italian, Byzantine and Moorish themes from southern Spain and France. Arches and casement windows are often featured. Patios, courtyards, balconies and loggias harken the Mediterranean climate. Its elaborate details include parapets, twisted columns and pediments. Steel-troweled stucco walls, red tile roofs, wrought iron grilles and railings and wood brackets and balconies serve as the style's materials. Oolitic (or sedimentary) limestone, ceramic tile and terra cotta are used for ornamentation. Applied Spanish baroque decoration generously surrounds openings, balconies and cornices.

The Hacienda's exterior stucco, in "hump and bump" design, was applied by the original plasterers, who were inspired by mullet leaping from the nearby Pithlachascotee River. The hotel's pink or coral color can be described as an orange-pink or pink-orange color.

THE HACIENDA'S ARCHITECT

Architect Thomas Reed Martin (1866–1949) was brought to Florida by one of the state's major developers during the turn of the twentieth century. In an impressive forty-year career in Florida, Martin designed five hundred residences, commercial buildings and public and private buildings in Tampa, Sarasota, Fort Myers, Nokomis and New Port Richey. Many of Martin's buildings are listed in the National Register of Historic Places, and he was posthumously honored as a Great Floridian in 2000.

Martin demonstrated a Modernist interpretation of the Mediterranean Revival style. His designs reflected modern streamline forms embellished with Mediterranean Revival features, similar in spirit to the designs of Irving Gill, whose residential architecture in Southern California was transitional between the Mediterranean Revival and the more modern style of the West Coast.

Born in Menasha, Wisconsin, Martin relocated with his family to Chicago, where he was employed as a draftsman with Global Machinery Company and later apprenticed with the prestigious architectural firm Holabird and Roche.

While at the firm, Martin met Chicago socialite and art patron Bertha Palmer (1849–1918), the widow of Chicago real estate developer Potter Palmer and the owner of the Palmer House Hotel. Among her more important efforts aimed at gender equity, Bertha Palmer invented the brownie dessert in the Palmer House Hotel's kitchen and debuted the confection at the Columbian Exposition World's Fair in 1893, for which she served as chair of the board of "lady managers" and the main organizer of the Woman's Building.

Palmer commissioned Holabird and Roche to design her large winter home in Sarasota, Florida. At the time, she was the largest landholder in the Sarasota and Lake Myakka areas and became renowned for her real estate developments and the introduction of revolutionary agricultural and ranching practices in Florida.

In the fall of 1910, at the age of forty-four, Martin arrived in Osprey to spend his winter overseeing the construction of the Oaks, Bertha Palmer's costly seasonal home at Historic Spanish Point on Little Sarasota Bay. The socialite never built Martin's original design, preferring his alternative sketches for a more modest winter residence. Palmer amassed eighty thousand acres, on which she established a model cattle ranch, Meadow Sweet Pastures, and launched a homestead colony.

Martin Relocates to the Sunshine State

Martin became enamored of the region and its prospects and returned to Chicago in 1911 to gather his wife, daughter and three sons to relocate to Florida. He first operated the Martin Building and Mercantile Company in Venice (today's Nokomis), where the post office was housed and where he briefly served as the postmaster.

In 1922, Martin was awarded a contract for Dr. Fred Albee's development plans in Nokomis, including the construction of the first of several modern bungalows built in Nokomis in the Spanish-Italian style. The homes were built on speculation for sale as winter homes. Additionally, Martin designed the Pollyanna Inn, which was demolished in 1972.

Martin's other commission was the design of Albee's personal winter home in Nokomis, known as Point of Palms, on a large waterfront parcel; it was completed in 1923 for $50,000.

Martin then relocated to Sarasota, where he opened his own practice, Martin and Hosmer Studios, with architect Clare Hosmer, maintaining offices in Fort Myers and Sarasota. The partnership lasted only until February 1925.

Thomas Reed Martin's career flourished during the Florida land boom of the 1920s. Among the five hundred homes Martin designed in the Sarasota area, many are considered Floridian-style homes, typified by glass block and embellished formed concrete. Martin's Mediterranean Revival home on North Palm Avenue, designed for L.D. Reagin, the owner and publisher of the *Sarasota Times*, still stands as Zak's Prime Steakhouse.

One of Martin's best-known projects in Sarasota was Burns Court, a collection of Spanish bungalows off Pineapple Avenue built for prominent developer Owen Burns. Martin also designed the William J. Burns House (Burns was the founder of the International Detective Agency) on Sarasota Bay and the Case House, both on South Washington Boulevard in St. Armands Key. Both residences are listed in the National Register of Historic Places.

Martin created the original sketches for the home of John and Mable Ringling, Cà d' Zan, but Martin declined a fee reduction proposed by John Ringling, and the couple selected a competing design by Dwight James Baum and built by Owen Burns.

The architect's own private residence at 1855 Oak Street in Owen Burns's Washington Park neighborhood was completed and occupied in December 1926. Martin's three-bedroom, three-bath property included a detached

George R. Sims hired Thomas Reed Martin to design the Pasco building (1926) on the southeast corner of Grand Boulevard and Nebraska Avenue. *West Pasco Historical Society.*

guest suite with views of the swimming pool, heart-pine floors, pecky cypress beams in the living room, an arched entryway to the dining room and heart-pine stairs and railings.

"Every line speaks of the creative genius of its designer," gushed the *Sarasota Herald.* "This beautiful residence is regarded as one of the finest built this year…suggesting a bit of Old Spain." This description would later be used in advertisements for Martin's eventual work the Hacienda Hotel. Martin also designed four manor homes and about twenty smaller houses in Washington Park.

When the board of directors for the Hacienda Hotel asked Martin to design for New Port Richey his masterpiece, the architect had already designed Pollyann Inn (1922), renamed the Villa Nokomis, on the Tamiami Trail and the Mira Mar Hotel (1924) in Sarasota. The architect had also designed several significant structures and residences in New Port Richey.

In 1937, Martin and an unrelated architect, Clarence Augustine Martin, who had retired to Sarasota after serving as dean of the Architecture School at Cornell University, partnered in designing the Moderne Art Deco–styled Sarasota Municipal Auditorium, listed in the National Register of Historic Places as the Municipal Auditorium-Recreation Club. Completed in 1938 through the Works Project Administration as a federal economic stimulus project, the structure featured a truss system that supported a barrel-vaulted roof.

Above: The New Port Richey Chamber of Commerce displays Thomas Reed Martin's renderings of the exterior of the Hacienda Hotel. *West Pasco Historical Society.*

Left: Thomas Reed Martin's design for the hotel's lobby included a prominent fireplace and plaster and wood beams. *West Pasco Historical Society.*

After rebranding his firm as the Martin Studio of Architecture, Martin collaborated with his sons Frank C. Martin and Jerome K. Martin. The family firm designed the Moderne-styled, streamlined Chidsey Library (1941), which currently houses the Sarasota County History Museum and the Sarasota County Visitors' Bureau.

In the 1930s, Martin's firm also designed the expansion of the historic Columbia Restaurant in Ybor City, Tampa, originally opened by Casimiro Hernandez Sr. as a saloon in 1903 before it was rebranded and began serving meals in 1905. Martin's son Frank C. Martin collaborated with architect Ivo de Minicis of Rimini, Italy, with whom he designed other structures in Sarasota.

In addition to the Hacienda Hotel, New Port Richey proudly claims at least seven known Thomas Reed Martin designs: the Pasco building (1926), the Meighan Theatre (1926) and the private residences of Warren E. Burns (1926), James H. Becker (1926), Gene Sarazen (1928) and Thomas Meighan (1928). (See chapters 7, 9 and 13.)

Thomas Reed Martin died peacefully at his home in Sarasota's now-historic Granada subdivision on October 21, 1949, at the age of eighty-four. In his nearly forty years of practice in Sarasota, Martin contributed enormously to Florida's legacy of architectural and artistic design.

11

THE HACIENDA'S OPENING GALA IN 1927

By December 17, 1926, a full-page advertisement from the Burns-Becker Company encouraged patrons to reserve a room at The Hacienda, now expected to open in mid-January.

On Friday, February 4, 1927, the *New Port Richey Press* published a headline in large-point, bold capital letters and an article about the hotel's debut:

HACIENDA OPENS SATURDAY NIGHT
Hotel Ready for Public Inspection
City Club Banquet Planned as Formal Opening February 17
Guests Welcomed, Dining Room in Operation, Large Program of Functions
Planned for Season with Dinner Dance February 12ᵗʰ

The Hacienda, complete to the last detail and furnished throughout, is ready for occupancy and will be opened for dinner and a public inspection tomorrow night.

The new hotel is no less a gem of architecture and construction. Its furnishings bespeak the exercise of the taste of an artist.

The foyer of the hotel, the beautiful dining room, the color scheme and decorative features, and the softness of the lighting effects combine in an effect which will make the community-built hotel its own best advertisement.

The rooms are commodious, and the furnishings are the last word. Each room is fitted with a telephone. The suites are sumptuous. The hotel is a veritable cameo Ritz Carlton. New Port Richey's stock, the public will

The Hacienda Hotel looms over Orange Lake, circa 1927. *West Pasco Historical Society.*

agree on inspection of the hotel tomorrow, has taken a leap upward which could be caused by no other single piece of construction.

The program of festivities for the new hotel is already a large one. More than twenty guests will be ensconced in the rooms and suites by tomorrow night. The first fête planned for the hotel after tomorrow's inspection will be a dinner-dance to be held Saturday, February 12th with spaces for 150 guests. This function will be preliminary for the formal opening of the hotel planned for Thursday, February 17th, when New Port Richey's Civic Club will host at a banquet and entertainment. Places may be reserved for this banquet at a charge of $5 per plate.

The City Club [formerly the Civitan Club] banquet will be attended by dignitaries of the state and distinguished guests from many parts of the country. The affair will be an official commemoration of the opening of the hotel.

Arthur A. Boardman, manager of The Hacienda, today announces his executive staff. Ray Poole is assistant manager. Otto Harschart, who opened the dining room of the Mirasol at Davis Island, and a chef of more than twenty years' experience, has been engaged as head chef. He has as first assistant Harry Maya, whose Chinese dishes will be a feature of the cuisine. Bennett Mallard has been engaged as room clerk.

The *Tampa Sunday Tribune* announces the opening of the Hacienda Hotel in its issue on February 4, 1927. *West Pasco Historical Society.*

A First Glimpse of the Hacienda Hotel

On Saturday, February 5, two thousand excited individuals in formal evening attire passed through the hotel, inspecting the spacious halls, handsome lobby and elegant dining room as an orchestra provided music. Guests marveled at $30,000 worth of European furnishings purchased from the Tampa

Luxurious European furnishings from Tampa Hardware Company grace the Hacienda Hotel's lobby. *Published in* New Port Richey Press, *May 2, 1930; West Pasco Historical Society.*

Interior View of The Hacienda New Port Richey Fla.

Hardware Company. Hav-A-Tampa cigars, made of Cuban tobacco and hand rolled in Ybor City, were sold in the lobby. Madame Dorice Bowman sang, and the orchestra finished after midnight.

The public entered the hotel through its south entrance on Main Street. They stepped through a wrought iron gate and into an open, picturesque courtyard, currently graced by a bubbling fountain at its center. There, they marveled at the building's U-shaped edifice facing Main Street. Five wide arches extended the length of the building and opened to a long loggia. Three sets of double French doors with top-arched transoms accessed the wide, rectangular lobby. Above the five arches was a long covered veranda on the third floor, with a low parapet adorned by double wood columns with ornamental corbels near the roofline. The red clay barrel tile roof was visible above. South-facing guest rooms on the third floor overlooked the veranda and courtyard below.

Two wings of guest rooms, perpendicular to the entry and lobby beyond, extended on the east and west sides of the courtyard and projected toward Main Street. The lobby and west side dining room's high ceilings prevented a second floor above them, and the third floor existed only above those spaces. The west wing contained two floors and accessed the third floor, which extended to the east wing. The west wing's second story was accessible only through an entry in the courtyard.

The west wing's east side overlooked the courtyard and had four arches that opened to a long loggia connecting to the other one near the entry. The west wing's west side faced Sims Park and the river. The east wing's west side faced the courtyard but omitted arches and loggia. The east wing's east side faced Riverside Place Street (today's Bank Street). The two wings' front façades facing Main Street were asymmetrical. The west wing's façade featured a balcony on the second floor. On its third floor, the southeast corner suite contained a solarium facing the street. On the third floor's southwest corner was the open terrace of the east-facing guest room. The west wing's façade featured an open stucco staircase that wrapped around the corner, connecting the courtyard to the second floor.

The north side of the hotel overlooked Sims Park and featured four wide arches, behind which a ground-floor veranda extended nearly the length of the building and opened to a terrace connecting to Sims Park. The veranda also featured two sets of French doors with arched transoms that accessed the lobby. The third floor also featured a covered veranda, onto which the third-floor's north guest rooms faced. The north side also featured balconies, where the east and west wing corridors ended, facing the park. The east wing

Left: The recently completed Hacienda Hotel featured prominently in the *New Port Richey Press* on March 4, 1927. *West Pasco Historical Society.*

Below: The hotel's north veranda features outdoor furniture for guests' relaxation, circa 1927. *West Pasco Historical Society.*

featured an open bell tower that extended above the third floor. The guest room beneath the tower also featured a balcony. An open stucco staircase wrapped around the corner, connecting the ground-floor veranda to the third-floor veranda.

The dining room in the hotel's northwest corner featured three sets of French doors with arched transoms facing Sims Park and another three sets of French doors with arched transoms facing the river.

Upon their entry into the lobby, guests faced a massive limestone fireplace, a coat of arms above its mantel, flanked by two sets of French doors with arched transoms leading to the north veranda. Clusters of seven Mediterranean-style sofas in a floral-patterned upholstery and numerous armchairs provided conversation areas and opportunities for relaxation. The voluminous ceiling was adorned with ornamental plaster beams connecting to large, elaborate corbels on the stucco walls. Three Spanish wrought iron chandeliers with electric candles were suspended by ornamental chains from the ceiling. To the left—or west—a large, sweeping, wood-framed, segmented arch led to the dining room. To the right—or east—a framed arch was flanked by two sets of double arches, each joined by twisted columns. Stairs led through one double arch to the second floor. Ornamental iron grilles flanked each side of the stairs. The center arch led to the east entrance on Riverside Place.

The following morning, Tampa Bay area locals read about the grand opening in the *Tampa Morning Tribune*:

> *New Hacienda Hotel Greets Vacationists to New Port Richey*
> *Structure One of the Most Attractive in Well Known Resort*
> *Building Cost $100,000 and Furnishings Represent Outlay of $30,000*
>
> *It is easy for one who gets his first view of the Hacienda Hotel to wonder if he is in dreamland. In Florida many beauties are unveiled [by] those from the frozen north who come to visit us, but it is said nowhere in the state is there a more satisfying picture of a part of "old Spain" set down in such a natural beauty spot as surrounds the Hacienda Hotel, a name that is truly indicative of what it signifies.*
>
> *The story of the building of this hotel is a romance in itself. It is the outgrowth of the dream of a local citizen whose first conception was a city club building and which the dream was later, on account of the need, switched to a hotel building proposition. With the united support of the local Civitan club this dream became a fact and we now have in The*

The north elevation's arched veranda and tower exemplify Mediterranean Revival architectural motifs. *West Pasco Historical Society*.

Hacienda, a hotel second to none, regardless of cost, in the state. For its size, it is a complete conception of an ideal hotel.

Hotel Cost $100,000

The actual cost of the building, $100,000, was raised by the community and financed without outside help.

The furnishings represent $30,000 additional and the land on which the building stands was donated by Mr. and Mrs. James E. Meighan, and is valued at $50,000. Mr. Meighan is the brother of Thomas Meighan, movie star, with his wife and some friends are among the first guests of the hotel.

The building was erected, furnished and received its first guests in 184 days from the day of the breaking of ground, a record in itself in rapid high grade construction. The architect, Thomas Reed Martin, of Sarasota, has simply added in this hotel his masterpiece of many successful buildings.

The superintendent of construction, Oliver Le May, of St. Petersburg, has again shown his ability as a builder and contractor.

Has Attractive Lobby

Everyone concerned in the financing and construction of the hotel no matter in what capacity has done his part well. Arthur Boardman, manager of the hotel, is a man with years of experience in hotel work. He was connected with such well known hotels as the Biltmore, of New York, and the Ponce de Leon, of St. Augustine, and for several years was superintendent of service for the Chicago, Duluth, and Georgian Bay Transit Company of the "Great Lakes."

To Warren E. Burns and James H. Becker, it is generally agreed that more credit is due for the success of this enterprise than to any others. For months their time and money has been poured into the enterprise. It is a monument to their civic pride and forceful management.

The lobby of this hotel deserves a story in itself to properly describe its beauties. The hotel building is constructed with a patio 75 by 100 feet between two wings. Its setting is among the oaks, palms, hickory, and magnolias in their natural habitat on the banks of the turquoise blue Pithlachascotee River.

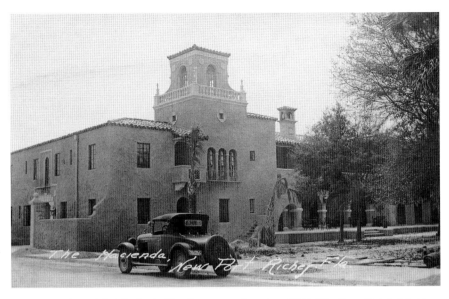

The completion of the Hacienda Hotel's construction, circa 1927. *West Pasco Historical Society*.

Snowbird Ed Wynn—formerly Thomas Meighan's next-door neighbor in Great Neck—served as the master of ceremonies at one of the grand-opening receptions held in November 1926. The film and radio comic expressed his great pleasure in visiting "the most beautiful city imaginable" and predicted the city "will attract some of the greatest people in the north." A large group gathered around Wynn in the hotel's foyer to witness the formal naming of the hotel.

A contemporaneous advertisement for The Hacienda capitalized on its lush location, modern amenities and moderate rates:

> *Set in the midst of nature's own beauty spot, on the banks of the Cotee River is this new, beautiful and modern hotel—containing 50 guest rooms, each with bath, all fitted with fixtures that satisfy the most exacting.*
>
> *A large Spanish lobby suitable for dinner dances and social functions of various kinds.*
>
> *The Hacienda offers to its guests a dining room service unexcelled—special features such as steam heat, telephone service in each room. Auto and boat service, horseback riding, fishing and many other forms of entertainment are part of the complete year-round service The Hacienda will render its guests.*
>
> *Reasonable rates will prevail.*

On Saturday, February 12, the hotel's management sponsored a dinner-dance with guests from Florida's west coast cities and visitors from the North. Music was provided by Blue Steel's Orchestra and the Sun Set Hills Country Club Orchestra on loan from the directors of the country club in Tarpon Springs.

The Hacienda hosted what would become the first annual Fireman's Ball, organized by the New Port Richey Volunteer Fire Department and attended by more than one hundred couples. The group named the first event George Washington's Birthday Ball, because on its date in 1927, Congress convened in a joint session to commemorate the birthday of the country's first president, leading to celebrations across the nation.

Luncheons, bridge parties, dinner parties and supper parties continued in quick succession through the hotel's inaugural month.

Coincidentally, five men with the first name of Richard were the first guests to sign The Hacienda's official guest registry. Richard Doran of New York was the first to sign. He was joined by four generations of the Ravenhall family: Richard Ravenhall of West Point, New York; Richard Ravenhall II and Richard Ravenhall III, both of New Port Richey; and Richard Ravenhall IV of West Point.

Wilson W. McIntyre (1850–1942), whose reputation included his patronage of every new business in the city, had the distinction of purchasing the first meal served in The Hacienda's dining room. Originally from Canada, McIntyre relocated from Maine to New Port Richey in 1912 and later proclaimed himself the second settler in the town, arriving a day after Frank Howard. As a master craftsman and cabinet maker, he manufactured cedar chests in a space in the rear of the post office in the Havens building.

On February 18, the *New Port Richey Press* announced:

Symphony of Gaiety, Beauty, Music Open Charming Hacienda

A double social christening introduced The Hacienda to the people of this city and neighboring cities within this past week.

The formal opening of the new hotel was held last night in the presence of 120 persons, with the City Club of New Port Richey as host, and with entertainment and a program of speeches which elevated the function to the premiere place in social festivities since the city was a settlement.

Saturday night past, nearly two hundred guests thronged the hotel at a dinner-dance where friends of New Port Richians from many cities of the west coast were notable. Last night's affair was essentially a New Port Richey gathering, when pioneers and newcomers to the city rubbed elbows and danced and played cards throughout a night of infinite enjoyment. Names of those who attended both functions will be published in the special souvenir edition of the New Port Richey Press, *scheduled for publication soon.*

A program of special merit was successfully carried out at the City Club party, due in great measure to the efforts of Charles F. Hoffman, president of the City Club, Mayor Edgar A. Wright, and the corps of aides. Mayor Wright responded to the toast "The City," propounded by Toastmaster Hoffman, after the toastmaster had introduced several notable persons of New Port Richey. The mayor's speech was a sincere expression of his affection for the city which has twice honored him with its highest office. He outlined the city's past and his hopes for the present and received a fine ovation.

Dr. W.W. Hunt, substituting on the program for George R. Sims, who was absent unavoidably from town, fell the lot of expressing the most popular sentiment of the evening....

[Hunt's] clever peroration to the pronouncement of the name "Jim" Becker, as the subject of his subject, was greeted with general approval, and when Mr. Becker's name was flung to the gathering, tribute was accorded with that "estimable citizen" which left no doubt of the place that lovable "Jim" has found in the heart of the community.

The entire gathering was on its feet in tribute to Mr. Becker when the doctor concluded his talk.

The unceasing surveillance by Mr. Becker of the construction of the hotel, his mind-taxing attention to scores of important details, his financial ownership of The Hacienda's birth, and the artistry of his taste, demonstrated by the beautiful appointments and furnishings of the new hotel, were called to attention of a hundred-odd friends of "Jim."

The same edition of the newspaper published The Hacienda's advertisement for "Sunday dinner/the west coast's finest hotel/$1.50." The dinner's fare included "Chicken from our own farms—Golden Waffles—Orange Blossom Honey—Other Dainty Dishes." Additionally, "Our à la Carte Menu is complete in every detail and our food perfection plus."

"The Hacienda will make New Port Richey," actor-composer-tailor Earl Benham told the press while attending the grand opening during his week's visit to the city following a week in Havana, Cuba. "It's almost unbelievable what a difference a first-class hotel has made in the city. And the news about the new golf course is most encouraging. It's certainly good to get back to town and our only regret is that the season for us this year will be brief."

Above: *New Port Richey Press* publishes a special Hacienda Hotel edition on March 4, 1927. *West Pasco Historical Society*.

Opposite: Henry Fletcher created a panoramic view of the hotel using frames from a 1929 home movie featuring George and Fannie Emerson. *West Pasco Historical Society*.

Benham was accompanied by his wife, actor Christine Mangasarian, "whose popularity here was ineradicably established last winter," according to the newspaper, and their son, Jimmie. During their visit, the couple was entertained by George and Marjorie Sims, attended a card party hosted by Joseph Foley and a city club banquet and sailed on the gulf in Warren E. Burns's yacht.

The Tampa Paint Company purchased an advertisement in the *New Port Richey Press* to honor Warren E. Burns, James H. Becker, Thomas Reed Martin and the artisans and craftsmen responsible for the hotel's construction:

> *We feel we are to be congratulated on having been selected by Messrs. Burns and Becker to superintend the decoration of their homes.*
>
> *We also feel that we owe a debt of gratitude to the community at large for the advertising that we are bound to get from the use of our materials in The Hacienda.*
>
> *When the architect of these buildings, Thomas Reed Martin, selected the materials manufactured by George D. Wetherill & Company, he made us duty-bound to see that the best materials were used for each and every purpose. In the hands of that finished artist, James Proudlove, the decorations are more than decorations, they are works of art.*

The *New Port Richey Press* produced a pictural edition dedicated to the hotel on March 4. Newspaper headlines announced "Hacienda Wins Social Place at Once, Elaborate Functions Mark First Month of Operation" and "Brilliant Festivities Open New Port Richey's New Hotel, The Hacienda, Club Host a Banquet and Dance for Hotel Debut."

By the fall of 1927, the hotel's rates were six dollars per day for a single room and eleven dollars per day for a double American plan, meaning the inclusion of three daily meals (breakfast, lunch and dinner) for the length of the stay. Advertisements inviting guests to "spend the winter in New Port

Famous hotel guests enjoy a horseback excursion. *Left to right*: George Sims, Earl Benham, Gene Sarazen, Mary Sarazen, Christine Mangasarian Benham, Marjorie Sims and an unknown equine attendant. *West Pasco Historical Society, restored by No Naked Walls Art and Frame Shop.*

Richey" pridefully boasted a recent inspection by State Hotel Commissioner Bostain, who rated The Hacienda 99 percent, "nearly perfect as it is possible for a hostelry to attain."

Through the end of the 1920s and into the 1930s, The Hacienda's guest register books collected the signatures of its famous visitors, becoming veritable catalogues of the Jazz Age's luminaries of the stage, screen, music and literature.

12

THE LEGEND OF GLORIA SWANSON IN NEW PORT RICHEY

The Quintessential Glamor Girl Who Ruled Hollywood's Golden Age

There is no greater New Port Richey legend than that of grand dame actor Gloria Swanson. Her name has become synonymous with The Hacienda. But is the legend true?

DID SHE, OR DIDN'T SHE?

Locals hoped Gloria Swanson would join her friend Thomas Meighan in New Port Richey and anticipated her eventual arrival. According to historian Dr. Wilfred T. Neill, the petite but larger-than-life actor detested being dwarfed by large entries. Therefore, Thomas Reed Martin designed two small arches over the grand stairs that led down into The Hacienda's lobby to allow for Swanson's majestic entrance.

If you read the historical marker displayed at the Gloria Swanson Parking Lot facing the east side of the Hacienda Hotel, you will learn she visited the charming city and built a home on the Cotee River. However, is that truth or part of the legend of this glamorous silent screen star?

Who Was She?

Gloria Swanson (1899–1983) was an acclaimed silent screen actor during the 1910s and 1920s who retired young and later had a glorious comeback portraying a fading, long-forgotten silent screen star Norma Desmond in director Billy Wilder's classic *Sunset Boulevard* (1950), widely considered the greatest film noir ever produced. You've heard her famous lines from this film: "We didn't need voices, we had faces!" and "Mr. DeMille, I'm ready for my close-up." Younger audiences will recall the actor portraying herself in the disaster film *Airport 1975* (1974).

How Did She Get Her Start?

While touring Essanay Studios during a visit to Chicago, fourteen-year-old Swanson precociously asked if she could appear in a crowd scene. She was promptly hired as an extra and soon played bit roles in comedies, working alongside icon Charlie Chaplin in the short film *His New Job* (1915). After her parents separated in 1916, Swanson and her mother moved to Hollywood, where Swanson got a job at Mack Sennett's Keystone Company.

Her Personal Drama

Swanson married fellow Sennett actor Wallace Beery, best known for his later performance in the Oscar-winning all-star cast of *Grand Hotel* (1932). In her autobiography, Swanson later revealed that her new husband had become intoxicated on their wedding night and raped her. After discovering she had become pregnant, Beery allegedly deceived Swanson into drinking a concoction that induced an abortion.

When Did She Reach Stardom?

After establishing herself as a bathing beauty and comedienne, Swanson left Sennett for Famous Players–Lasky (later Paramount Pictures) and

Gloria Swanson (1899–1983). *PICRYL public domain archive, Get Archive LLC (public domain).*

achieved greatness in powerful director Cecil B. DeMille's series of sophisticated comedies, such as *Male and Female* (1919), costarring Thomas Meighan; *Don't Change Your Husband* (1919); and *Why Change Your Wife?* (1920), again costarring Meighan. She often portrayed tempestuous characters, wearing elaborate feather boas and jeweled headdresses.

Swanson branched out and performed in a series of films with director Sam Wood, including *Under the Lash* (1921), *Her Gilded Age* (1922) and *Beyond the Rocks* (1922), which also starred her friend Rudolph Valentino. Swanson's tumultuous offscreen life mirrored her onscreen life. After she married restaurateur Herbert Somborn, he discovered her affair with director Marshall Neilan and filed for divorce, alleging her adultery with thirteen men. This public scandal resulted in an "morals clause" addendum to her studio contract.

Swanson smartly established her own motion picture production company and performed in her own films, such as *Sadie Thompson* (1928), *Queen Kelly* (1929) and her first sound film, *The Trespasser* (1929). She was nominated for the first Academy Award for Best Actor for her performance in *Sadie Thompson* and received another nomination for her performance in *The Trespasser*. Tiring of the poor scripts that were available, she retired young from the films in 1941 and started business ventures outside the industry.

Her Alleged Affair with Joseph P. Kennedy

Those checking in to the Hacienda Hotel today may hear lore about the Gloria Swanson/Joe Kennedy Suite and question the link between the histrionic actor and the father of the thirty-fifth president. In her autobiography, *Swanson on Swanson*, published nearly two decades after Kennedy's death, Swanson alleged she had an affair with Joseph P. Kennedy Sr., whom President Franklin Delano Roosevelt appointed chair of the United States Maritime Commission and later ambassador to the Court of St. James, the United States' representative to Great Britain. Swanson alleged the illicit romance started with a kiss in the drawing room of a railroad car that was en route to Palm Beach, Florida, in 1928, and later necessitated the intervention of a Roman Catholic cardinal in Boston.

In the decade prior to his political career, Kennedy purchased a small film studio, Film Booking Offices of America (or FBO), which specialized in westerns, and the Keith-Albee-Orpheum (KAO) theater chain. By 1928, he had formally merged FBO and KAO to form Radio-Keith-Orpheum (RKO Studios). During this period, Swanson engaged the married Catholic father of eight children (the last, Teddy, was born in 1932) as her financial advisor. Shortly thereafter, Kennedy personally bankrolled her next picture.

In her memoir, Swanson publicly disclosed their first intimate encounter. Kennedy arrived at her hotel room and slowly closed the door behind him:

> *He moved so quickly that his mouth was on mine before either of us could speak. With one hand he held the back of my head, with the other he stroked my body and pulled at my kimono. He kept insisting in a drawn-out moan, "No longer, no longer. Now." He was like a roped horse, rough, arduous, racing to be free. After a hasty climax he lay beside me, stroking my hair. Apart from his guilty, passionate mutterings, he had still said nothing cogent.*

When Kennedy contemplated maintaining his marriage while engaged in a second household with Swanson, Cardinal William O'Donnell intervened. The clergyman told Swanson that such an arrangement would be as impossible as Kennedy divorcing, and the married father—in the words of the actor—"was exposing himself to scandal every time he so much appeared in public with me."

Despite local lore, there is no record of the couple ever tempestuously trysting at The Hacienda—or New Port Richey for that matter. But allegedly, Kennedy's obsession with Swanson drove him to travel to Europe with his wife, Rose, only to meet Swanson there. The three interacted, and Rose reportedly displayed no hint of knowledge about the affair. Kennedy lived in a primary residence in Massachusetts and had a winter estate on Ocean Drive in Palm Beach on Florida's east coast.

The Comeback

In 1950, Swanson made a historic return as fading silent screen actor Norma Desmond in the highly acclaimed *Sunset Boulevard*, for which she received her third Oscar nomination. According to columnist Bill Soberances, "she came back after a period of oblivion like the reappearance of Halley's Comet."

Director Cecil B. DeMille portrayed himself in the film. In a bit of brilliant casting, Austrian American director, screenwriter, actor and producer Eric von Stroheim portrayed Swanson's devoted butler. Von Stroheim was hailed as an avant-garde, visionary director of the silent era whose 1924 classic *Greed* is arguably one of the most important films ever made. In a pivotal scene in *Sunset Boulevard,* he operates the projector while screening for Norma and her younger lover (William Holden) one of Norma's old silent films—the film used is actually *Queen Kelly*, which von Stroheim directed—starring Swanson. With direct allusions like this, many believed Swanson was portraying herself, but nothing was further from the truth.

Although she appeared in a few later films, Swanson devoted most of the remainder of her career to television and theater. In her 1980 autobiography, *Swanson on Swanson*, the gracefully aging actor disclosed her long-term affair with Joseph Kennedy, who was then long deceased. She also claimed she accompanied Kennedy and his wife, Rose, on a cruise during the secret affair. Unstable in her relationships, Swanson was married six times, approaching Elizabeth Taylor's record.

What Is the Truth of Swanson Living in New Port Richey?

Swanson and Thomas Meighan were employees of Paramount Studios and appeared in several films together. Local newspapers reported on Swanson's multiple anticipated visits to New Port Richey as a friend and guest of Meighan. Reportedly, these visits were canceled due to various barriers. Newspapers also reported Swanson had invested in property in New Port Richey. However, when asked in an interview decades later, Swanson stated she never visited the city nor invested in property here. So, until we uncover a deed or record of her purchase of property, Gloria's word answers the question.

How Did the Rumors Start?

The rumors stem from a series of newspaper articles that report Gloria Swanson was part of a syndicate that purchased property in New Port Richey and had made plans to visit her land. However, there is no documentation of a visit, a deed or the construction of a home related to the actor. Let's follow the trail of what is documented in the press.

On January 11, 1930, the *Tampa Morning Tribune* announced:

> *Picture Star Plans to Visit New Pt. Richey*
> *Gloria Swanson May Look Over Her Lot*
>
> *They are looking for Gloria Swanson at New Port Richey during the early part of the season—and if she goes there they'll need more than traffic cops in that part of the state.*
>
> *Gloria owns some property in that beauty spot of Florida, close by the home of Tom Meighan, the big film star. And now, Leon Carrol, described recently by Ambassador Dawes as the funniest man in the world, is going to build a fine home, close to Tom's palace and Gloria's lot.*
>
> *Word of the expected arrival of Gloria was brought to Tampa yesterday by John W. Parkes, editor of the* New Port Richey Press, *a sprightly newspaper that keeps abreast with the growing city.*
>
> *When Gloria arrives there'll be big times in New Port Richey and for a time the big star of Tom Meighan will be temporarily dimmed. Tom can't shine against a woman like Gloria, and he wouldn't if he could, says editor Parkes.*

On January 11, 1930, the *Evening Independent* reported:

> *New Port Richey, Jan. 11—(AP)—Gloria Swanson, motion picture star, was expected to arrive here within the next few days to be the guest of Mr. and Mrs. Thomas Meighan, at their Jasmin Point home. Leon Errol and wife have been here since their return from England recently, and Madeline Cameron, Broadway musical comedy star, arrived yesterday.*

On January 8, 1930, the *Tampa Tribune* reported:

> Hell Harbor *to Be Shown Here Jan. 26*
> *Tom Meighan/Gloria Swanson May Attend*

The world premiere of Hell Harbor, *all-talking motion picture produced last summer on Rocky Point* [Tampa] *by Inspiration-United Artists studios under the direction of Henry King and a cast including Lupe Velez, Jean Hersholt, John Holland and other stars, is scheduled at the Tampa Theatre Sunday, January 26, according to a telegram received yesterday from Lou Lusty, studio press agent.*

In his wire to the chamber of commerce, Mr. Lusty urged Trenton C. Collins and other Tampans identified with the picture to arrange for personal appearances by Thomas Meighan and Gloria Swanson, who are expected to be at New Port Richey.

Miss Swanson is expected to arrive on the west coast within a few days and Mr. Meighan will be asked to escort the actress to the premiere.

It seems hardly likely that Swanson attended, as Meighan stole the spotlight when the film premiere took place on January 24—and it had been said, "Tom can't shine against a woman like Gloria, and he wouldn't if he could." The most compelling evidence that Swanson skipped the event is a large photograph that was published by the *Tampa Tribune* in its edition dated January 25, 1930. The image depicts Thomas Meighan in a tuxedo at the premiere under the headline "Tampans Give Ovation to *Hell Harbor* at Triumphal Premiere/Brought First Movie Premiere to Tampa." The article makes no mention of Gloria Swanson. Had she attended, there is no doubt the media would have reported it.

The final contemporaneous mention of Gloria Swanson and New Port Richey appears in the *Tampa Morning Tribune* from September 4, 1932:

Thomas Meighan is returning to New Port Richey around Christmas and reports from that attractive resort yesterday indicated that a number of big wigs of the movies, blondes and brunettes, will be there during the season. Gloria Swanson is or was—one gets one's senses strangely mixed in these days of property turn-backs—on the tax roll and was due last year, but something kept her away.

Further evidence came from professional golfer Gene Sarazen, who resided in the city during the era Swanson would have visited. In an article in the *St. Petersburg Times* from January 13, 1993, staff writer Robert Keefe quoted the credible Sarazen as saying, "She didn't spent [*sic*] any time there. She may have spent some time in West Palm Beach, but not in New Port Richey. I lived there."

Don't tell this to the locals. The city named a municipal parking lot after Swanson and erected signage with the inscription: "A renowned actress of the silent screen, Gloria Swanson was one of the colorful residents of New Port Richey during the Boom Era of the 1920s. The home she lived in can still be seen on the banks of the Cotee River."

"We lived like kings in queens in those days—and why not?" Swanson remarked on her experience in the limelight. "We were in love with life. We were making more money than we ever dreamed existed, and there was no reason to believe it would ever stop."

Gloria Swanson was a strong, intelligent woman who knew when to discreetly step back and, strategically, when to gloriously return.

13

NEW PORT RICHEY'S GOLF SUPERSTAR GENE SARAZEN

His Shot Heard Around the World in the 1935 Masters Remains the Sport's Most Famous Stroke Ever Played

He was the first of four men to achieve a Grand Slam by winning all four of golf's major professional golf championships. He won the U.S. Open in 1922 and 1932; the Professional Golfers' Association (PGA) Championship in 1922, 1923 and 1933; the British Open in 1932; and the Masters in 1935.

He won seven major championships, three before the age of twenty-two, making him the second-youngest winner of the event.

He was a member of six Ryder Cup biennial men's golf competition teams from 1927 to 1937.

He made a tremendous comeback with the four-wood "shot heard around the world"—the most famous golf shot in history—acing the double-eagle, three strokes under par, at the fifteenth hole at Augusta Nationals, later known as the Masters.

He invented the sand wedge golf club, considered one of the greatest advances in golf club technology, while residing in New Port Richey in 1931 and used it to win the British Open the following year. He later invented the interlocking grip used by Jack Nicklaus.

At the age of seventy-one, he played the British open and aced the Postage Stamp hole at Troon in his last tournament.

And he wintered at the Hacienda Hotel in New Port Richey, where he eventually built a home.

Gene Sarazen (1902–1997) was the golf legend responsible for many monumental sports achievements. At five feet, four inches tall while wearing his customary 1920s knickers on the course for the entirety of his life,

Left: Gene Sarazen (1902–1999). *PICRYL public domain archive, Get Archive LLC (public domain)*.

Opposite: Gene and Mary Peck Sarazen spent winters in New Port Richey. *PICRYL public domain archive, Get Archive LLC (public domain)*.

Sarazen was known as the "Squire" and was described as a fiery personality and a colorful performer. According to the *New York Times*, Sarazen's "stylish, effective swing and dogged demeanor" made him one of the greatest golfers of all time.

Born Eugenio Saraceni to poor Sicilian immigrants in Harrison, New York, Sarazen dropped out of school in the sixth grade to help support his family. At the age of eight, in 1910, he caddied at Larchmont Country Club and played golf on a makeshift neighborhood course using tin cups and wooden-shafted clubs.

Saraceni spent much of his time at the golf course in Bridgeport's Beardsley Park, where golf pro Al Ciuci introduced him to Brooklawn Country Club. After Saraceni impressed influential Brooklawn members with his prowess on the course, Archie and William Wheeler urged their golf pro, George Sparling, to hire him in the pro shop, where he worked as a club maker. After changing his name from Eugenio Saraceni (which he decided better suited a violinist or an opera singer rather than an athlete) to

Gene Sarazen, he entered the professional circuit, which was then dominated by Scottish and English players.

At twenty, in 1922, Sarazen won the U.S. Open in Skokie, Illinois, shooting 68 in the final round, the first golfer to shoot under 70 to win, defeating golf great Bobby Jones. With bravado, he challenged golf's showman Walter Hagen to a seventy-two-hole event for the 1923 World PGA Championship at Oakmont and won later that year. In 1932, Sarazen won the British Open at Sandwich and then the U.S. Open in Fresh Meadow for a historic double triumph in the world's two major Open Championships. In 1933, he added a third PGA win at Blue Mound in Wisconsin.

Previously engaged to actor Pauline Garon, Sarazen courted and proposed to Mary Peck of Springfield, Massachusetts, in January 1924. While he was a basketball player, Sarazen met Mary at a department store when the fourteen-year-old girl made an appearance on a raised dais after she was judged the winner of a Mary Pickford lookalike contest at a Springfield theater. Pickford, the first movie star, became "America's sweetheart" and was known for her long, curly tresses, which contributed to her frequent portrayal of youthful women.

Sarazen spent the day with Mary Peck and left Springfield with her photograph. Years later, in Florida, he coincidentally collided with Peck, who was then eighteen and visiting Miami with her parents in the family's winter home—but she did not recognize the now golfer. The couple married in June 1924 and sailed for Europe for their honeymoon.

Sarazen's Residency in New Port Richey

At a luncheon at The Hacienda on May 13, 1927, Sarazen discussed the possibilities of developing a Jasmin Point Golf Course after a three-hour survey of the proposed site on the west bank of the river. "New Port Richey is the place to live," asserted the Squire from the hotel's window-lined grand dining room, "and I say this after seeing all of Florida. [It] will be a more attractive place to live when it has a fine golf course such as the folks here are planning. You can have the most beautiful course in the state over there across the river."

Sarazen had purchased from Warren E. Burns a residential plot at Jasmin Point on River Road opposite the property owned by Thomas Meighan that was then currently under construction. Although the property was not located on the Pithlachascotee's riverbank, it had a magnificent, unobstructed view of the river.

Concurrent with plans for building a home, Sarazen signed a contract whereby he would supervise the construction of the new Jasmin Point Golf Club and manage it, and his entries in all the winter golf tournaments would now carry New Port Richey's name as his home course.

On November 3, 1927, the *New Port Richey Press* reported:

Work on Gene Sarazen Residence Started

Ground broke on November 3rd for a modern concrete building "of very pleasing [Mediterranean Revival] *design" and "not so pretentious as the mansion of Thomas Meighan being erected on an adjoining estate."*

H.A. Butler of Sarasota, the builder of Meighan's mansion, also won the bid for the Sarazen home, and Thomas Reed Martin, also of Sarasota, was the supervising architect. The local Hi-Test Products Company furnished the concrete tile building units.

Sarazen and his wife planned to arrive for permanent residence shortly after the Christmas holiday and occupy a suite at the Hacienda Hotel until the residence is completed, expected by February 1, 1928.

Sarazen's coming to New Port Richey, touted the local press, "will do as much to advertise this city and its superior attractions to the world as any other thing possibly could."

On December 20, 1927, the *Dade City Banner* reported:

Mr. and Mrs. Gene Sarazen arrived at New Port Richey this morning and are stopping at the Hotel Hacienda. Mr. and Mrs. Sarazen will remain at The Hacienda until their beautiful home, which they are building at Jasmin Point, is completed. The contractors are rushing the work and expect to have their home completed so that Mr. and Mrs. Sarazen will be able to move by the 15th of January. When their home is completed it will be one of the most attractive places in this vicinity. It faces the river and has

The Sarazen Estate at Jasmin Point, designed by Thomas Reed Martin, survives today. *West Pasco Historical Society.*

> *an excellent view both up and down the river and is across the street from the wonderful residence that Thomas Meighan is building. The home, with its wonderful surroundings, being located in the beautiful subdivision of Jasmin Point, is not only attractive but unusual. The architect has planned one room especially for Gene Sarazen to keep his golf clubs and trophies which he has won in past tournaments and will win in future ones. This is an unusually attractive room and will permit the display of the many wonderful cups that Gene Sarazen has won in the last few years.*

Thomas Reed Martin's architectural design featured prominent niches to conspicuously display Sarazen's golf clubs and numerous trophies in a home that was estimated to cost $20,000, roughly $352,000 in 2024. The two-story home had many of Martin's signature Mediterranean Revival touches, including a sunken living room and master bath, hand-painted Spanish tiles, coved ceilings, arches, balconies and twisted columns.

Sarazen as Manager of the Jasmin Point Golf Club

On May 10, 1927, Sarazen arrived in New Port Richey and met with City Club planners to discuss designs for an exclusive golf course and club. George Sims, James H. Burns and Warren E. Becker had recruited Sarazen

Gene Sarazen and actor Thomas Meighan on the Jasmin Point Golf Course, New Port Richey. *West Pasco Historical Society.*

to design the golf course for the average player and contracted him to manage the club during the winter months and provide professional golf instructions to its members. Frank Steele assisted in the design, representing Burns, who conceived and financially backed the project.

The nine-hole Jasmin Point Golf Course opened in February 1929, extending from the Pithlachascotee River west across the present U.S. Highway 19, south of the bridge into Port Richey. Avery Road and Astor Road bisect the site where most of the course formerly existed, the lake hazard today remaining behind the Richey Motel.

The ninth hole cut behind what was later Ho Ho Chinese Restaurant on U.S. Highway 19, where a pond is the only reminder of the now-defunct course. The proposed clubhouse, constructed for $38,000 on the riverside of the course, was to be near a saltwater swimming pool in the fairway and spacious tennis courts.

Mary Sarazen plays a round of golf with Flora Zabelle on the Jasmin Point Golf Course, New Port Richey. *West Pasco Historical Society.*

Despite the course's shortcomings, Sarazen and his wife, Mary, posed for photographs while golfing with actors Thomas Meighan, Flora Zabelle and Christine Mangasarian Benham.

The Golf Pro as Resident

Despite his celebrity status, Sarazen warmly mingled with city's residents and popularized golf among the local youth, frequently giving away golf clubs. Hoping to interest youth in the sport, Sarazen participated in the development of a small golf course around Orange Lake specifically for children to play on. Local youth cheered the superstar, who was frequently seen driving through town in a luxurious open touring automobile.

Sarazen's miniature golf course surrounding Orange Lake promotes the sport to city residents, circa 1932. *West Pasco Historical Society.*

On January 24, 1930, Sarazen transformed his 295 strokes in the seventy-two-hole first annual Agua Caliente Open in Tijuana, Mexico, for the $10,000 first prize, the largest purse to date. Three days later, his triumphant homecoming, declared a holiday with the schools closed, drew two thousand adoring welcomers. After arriving at the train depot in Tarpon Springs, Sarazen drove to New Port Richey, where he was met at the city limits by a band and a mile-long parade of festively bedecked automobiles. At a celebratory reception, George Sims served as the master of ceremonies, with congratulatory speeches by Mayor Charles W. Barnett, Warren E. Burns and Thomas Meighan.

INVENTION OF THE SAND WEDGE IN NEW PORT RICHEY

Sarazen was the ingenious inventor of the sand wedge in 1931, and it is used today. Previously, golf clubs had narrow blades, which prevented golfers from playing consistent shots from the bunker, commonly called "traps." The first golf courses were built on sand links land, and pits appeared, which were called "bunkers." Getting the ball out of a bunker was an arduous chore.

Sarazen spent four to five hours each day soldering various iron prototypes at the Scofield-Huddleston Garage on the southeast corner of Grand Boulevard and Gulf Drive in New Port Richey before he perfected the design. The homemade sand wedge he used in his victory at the 1932 British Open is displayed at the United States Golf Association (USGA) Museum in Liberty Corner, New Jersey.

Golf in the Local Headlines

Full-page advertisements for the Hacienda Hotel featured concierge arrangements for guests to use the new Jasmin Point Golf Course, and Sarazen and Mary attended soirees at the hotel with Thomas and Frances Meighan and George and Marjorie Sims.

On January 27, 1928, the *Dade City Banner* reported that golfer Johnny Farrell was a guest of the Hacienda Hotel and that he and Gene Sarazen had a match game in Clearwater. Farrell was voted America's Best Golf Professional in 1927 and 1928, after a winning streak at six consecutive tournaments.

In February 1931, the *St. Petersburg Times* reported Lester Rice, the golf editor of the *New York American*, had registered at The Hacienda as the latest of an increasing array of golf talent "destined to compete for the mythical and rather elusive crown of golf stardom on the Jasmin Point golf course." He received a hearty welcome from Sarazen, Meighan, Al Ciuci (the professional golfer who introduced Sarazen to the sport in 1917) and George Ade, a writer.

On March 16, 1933, Thomas and Frances Meighan and Gene and Mary Sarazen arrived in New Port Richey for a monthlong vacation. Sarazen rested and conditioned himself for the British Open.

The sweet glory of the golf pro tutoring locals on the course soured in only a few years.

According to an Associated Press news story from October 20, 1932, Sarazen filed in federal courts two $40,000 damage suits to collect for three years of service as a professional golf instructor at the Jasmin Point Golf Club. One of the suits was directed against the club corporation and the other was against his neighbor Warren E. Burns, who headed the club and Jasmin Point Estate, a corporation that sold lots adjacent to the golf course.

The lawsuits were based on a contract signed between Sarazen and the club in 1927, which guaranteed him an income of $20,000 for three years beginning on January 1, 1928. Sarazen contended the income failed to materialize. Representatives of the golf club contended that Sarazen broke the contract through his failure to carry out his obligations to sell signed golf balls, clubs, land and homes for the benefit of the club.

The Jasmin Point Club opened days after the great stock market crash of 1929 and closed during the Great Depression, and Sarazen sold his home in 1934. The couple eventually settled in Marco Island, Florida, where Mary made headlines as the first women to ever score a hole in one on the Marco Island Country Club course in 1967.

Despite Sarazen severing his ties with the area and relocating farther south, through the 1980s, a sign announcing Pasco County as the home of Gene Sarazen welcomed drivers as they exited Hillsborough County on Gunn Highway.

14

RAYMOND HITCHCOCK
AND FLORA ZABELLE

Today, in an enlarged framed photograph in the private dining room of The Hacienda, Flora Zabelle (1880–1968) sits at center on the hotel's terrace in January 1928, surrounded by Reginald and Marjorie Sims, Earl and Christine Benham and Gene and Mary Sarazen. Zabelle, with her dark features and piercing eyes, appears to be holding court. Who was this interesting-looking woman who graced the hotel nearly one hundred years ago?

Born Zabelle Mangasarian of Armenian descent in Constantinople, Ottoman Empire (now Istanbul, Turkey), Flora achieved national acclaim as a stage and silent film actor. Flora's father, Dr. Mangasar Magurditch Mangasarian, was an American rationalist and secularist who wrote hundreds of essays and lectures on religious criticism and the philosophy of religion. In 1900, he organized the Independent Religious Society of Chicago, a rationalist group, of which he remained the pastor until 1925. Dr. Mangasarian also joined the prohibition movement and wrote and lectured on the ills of liquor.

During the Hamidian massacres of the 1890s, Dr. Mangasarian; his wife, Akaby Christine; his son, Arman; and Flora, age three, immigrated to the United States. Flora's sister, Christine Mangasarian Benham, would also become an actor.

At the age of nineteen, Flora relocated to New York with the ambition to pursue a theatrical career. She auditioned for producer Henry W. Savage, who was organizing a second Castle Square Grand Opera Company, and joined the chorus.

NEW PORT RICHEY'S HACIENDA HOTEL

In her Broadway debut in 1900, Zabelle portrayed Poppy in *San Toy*. In 1902, she appeared in the film *King Dodo*. While she continued to perform on stage, she transitioned to film after marrying actor Raymond Hitchcock.

Flora's remarkable story of immigration from the east and her emancipation through education and a career captured the attention of the American media. In 1913, the *Ogden Standard* dedicated a full page to Flora with the title "Out of a Harem to Fight for Woman Suffrage in America":

> *In all this fair land, there isn't another woman who represents "emancipation" to such a degree as Flora Zabelle.…She is the very symbol of "throw convention and customs to the winds."…She broke the chrysalis of tradition and in the gorgeous colors of the butterfly, raised her wings and flew away to freedom, shouting "emancipation."*

Zabelle's film appearances included parts in *A Village Scandal* (1915), costarring Raymond Hitchcock and Fatty Arbuckle; *The Ringtailed Rhinoceros* (1915), costarring Hitchcock; *The Red Widow* (1916), costarring John Barrymore and distributed by Paramount Pictures; and *A Perfect 36* (1918), starring Mabel Normand and distributed by Goldwyn Pictures.

Zabelle appears in a photograph dated January 30, 1927, with Frank and Bertha Case, Emil Jannings, Jesse Lasky and Carl Van Vechten at Famous Players–Lasky Corporation, which changed its name to Paramount Pictures later that year. Jannings appears in costume on the set of *The Way of All Flesh* (1927), for which he received the first Academy Award for Best Actor. Case was an author who owned and managed the Algonquin Hotel during the heyday of the Algonquin Round Table, a group of New York City writers, critics, actors and wits; he visited the Hacienda Hotel in 1934. Van Vechten was a writer and artistic photographer.

In May 1905, Zabelle married the charismatic actor Raymond Hitchcock, who was fifteen years her senior. The union continually made dramatic national headlines from the announcement of their marriage until Hitchcock's death in 1929.

Flora Zabelle and Raymond Hitchcock were the Jennifer Lopez and Ben Affleck of the early twentieth century. The roller-coaster relationship was rocked by charges against Hitchcock for sexually abusing two girls (for which he was acquitted after he began serving a prison sentence), a house fire, gossip of infidelity, separations, reconciliations and, finally, Raymond's sudden death in Flora's arms.

Left: Flora Zabelle (Mrs. Raymond Hitchcock, 1880–1968). *PICRYL public domain archive, Get Archive LLC (public domain).*

Right: Raymond Hitchcock (1865–1929). *PICRYL public domain archive, Get Archive LLC (public domain).*

Raymond Hitchcock (1865–1929) was a lean, raspy and deep-voiced actor and stage producer who appeared in and produced thirty plays on Broadway from 1898 to 1928. He toured the nation in *Hitchy-Koo*, his most successful revue, a collaboration with Cole Porter that played to packed audiences at George C. Cohan and Sam H. Harris's theater in New York. Hitchcock also transitioned to silent films in the 1920s while continuing his glorious career on the stage.

Personifying the public's image of an actor, Hitchcock dressed in extreme styles, wearing a pearl-gray derby, checkered suits, pearl-gray spats, diamond rings and cravats. The actor also drove a conspicuous automobile that was painted canary yellow.

Fellow actor Billy Van once accused Hitchcock of doing him harm by thinking evil thoughts about him. When the court dismissed the case, Hitchcock quipped to the reporters, "The only time I ever wished Van were dead was when I saw him trying to play Hamlet."

After graduating from high school in his hometown of Auburn, New York, Hitchcock worked as a shoe salesman until a member of the Auburn

Philharmonic Opera Club discovered him and cast him as Ko-Ko in *The Mikado*. After traveling as a member of the chorus for a professional touring show, Hitchcock resumed selling shoes. He returned to the stage as Sir Joseph in Gilbert and Sullivan's operetta *HMS Pinafore* and caught the attention of New York critic Alan Dale, who lauded the actor as "America's foremost operatic comedian."

Once producer Henry Savage offered Hitchcock a ten-year contract on the professional stage, the actor experienced a meteoric rise to fame, leading to a long, successful stage career alternating between dramatic roles and roles in comic operas. He also made several phonograph recordings.

Raymond Hitchcock. *Harris and Ewing photograph collection, Library of Congress Prints.*

Hitchcock endorsed Moxie Soda, which distributed promotional wooden figurines in his likeness for display in hotels and soda shops across the country. Once more popular than Coca-Cola, the brand was advertised to cure the "loss of manhood."

Performing in the title role in *King Dodo*, Hitchcock wrote to King Edward and referred to himself as the only man in America with the title of king. The monarch personally responded to this humorous note.

While Flora and Raymond performed in *The Yankee Council* in St. Louis, they surprised the cast by marrying, with the bride's father officiating. Although the couple had been engaged for some time, their contracts stipulated that they would each remain single during the theatrical season.

Flora joined Raymond in a three-story, nineteen-room estate in Great Neck, Long Island, called Allen Cines, built in 1904 for $45,000. A few years later, Raymond took up farming on a nearby 360-acre farm stocked with Holstein cattle, chickens and ducks.

For many years, Raymond lived at the Algonquin Hotel in New York and befriended its owner, Frank Case.

The Fugitive Comedian Accused of Child Abuse

In 1907, Zabelle and Hitchcock experienced a national scandal when the latter was charged with the sexual abuse of two adolescent girls. The charges also implicated New York magnate and former congressman William Astor Chanler and resulted in libel charges for the powerful newspaper publisher William Randolph Hearst. Readers of the *New York Times* followed the case for a year, just as a later generation would follow a similar case involving entertainer Michael Jackson in 1993–94.

Fraught with inconsistencies, the case involved allegations of an extortion conspiracy, efforts to induce the youths to testify against the actor and a mother's testimony exonerating the actor.

While performing in *The Yankee Tourist* at the Astor Theater in Manhattan in October 1907, Hitchcock was arrested on the charge of having assaulted and abducted fifteen-year-old Helen von Hagen in November 1906. The district attorney's office announced that other charges of a similar nature—involving other girls—would be presented to the grand jury. "I am thunderstruck," the actor exclaimed upon his arrest. His attorney proclaimed, "The arrest of Mr. Hitchcock is an outrage!" Hitchcock was arraigned on charges, under investigation by the New York Society for the Prevention of Cruelty to Children for nearly a year and released on $3,000 bail.

Three girls appeared as witnesses before the grand jury: Elsie Voecks, Flora Whiston and Helen von Hagen, ranging in age from twelve to fifteen.

The charges against Hitchcock were the result of the actor reporting to police that the adult brother of one of the girls had attempted to extort him. Hugo Voeck, the brother of Elsie Voeck, had approached Hitchcock at the Astor Theatre threatening to provide a story to the newspapers involving the actor and his sister unless the actor paid him to keep quiet. Shortly after Hitchcock reported the blackmail scheme, the actor was arrested on charges of abusing the girls. Voeck, who had devised a similar plot against William Astor Chanler, pleaded guilty to the charges of having attempted to extort $1,500 from Hitchcock.

Hitchcock's friend and neighbor in Great Neck William Astor Chanler brought charges of libel against William Randolph Hearst related to an article published in *Evening Journal* that reported Chanler was with Hitchcock in Chanler's automobile when two of the young girls were present. The article reported Hitchcock brought the girls to Great Neck and introduced them to Chanler during an abduction that lasted three days. More damaging to Hearst, the article stated the same story had been confirmed by two women.

Chanler testified the girls were never present in their company and that his runabout car could not accommodate a chauffeur, two adult men and two girls. Chanler also testified that he had never seen the girls before or in Hitchcock's presence in the actor's residence, car or boat.

In a dramatic turn of events befitting one of his theatrical plays or silent films, Hitchcock went missing on the morning after the court appearance in which he was charged with six indictments. According to Flora, he was headed to a Turkish bath after a sleepless night with only a few dollars in his pocket and wearing diamond rings.

When Hitchcock failed to attend a hearing, the judge forfeited bail. The case was adjourned until the actor's friends found him and returned him to court.

Hitchcock's distinctive features were so well known to the public that the police believed the actor could not have remained in New York for more than twenty-four hours without being detected. Police theorized he fled with two companions to Vermont, where he crossed the border to Canada, from which he could not be extradited.

Flora Zabelle bravely continued to perform in *The Yankee Tourist* with her husband's understudy, Wallace Beery, but she told detectives she feared her husband may have been kidnapped or murdered by a band of blackmailers who had been hounding him for months—or he had taken his own life.

A man fitting Hitchcock's description boarded the White Star Liner *Majestic* that was sailing to England, and authorities sent a telegram to the ship's captain instructing him to have the actor held by British police if he was found aboard.

A week after his disappearance, Hitchcock gave himself up to the authorities as his wife stood beside him in court. Claiming to have been ensconced in a New York hotel room and suffering an emotional breakdown from the stress of his circumstances, Hitchcock appeared pale and disturbed and not his "jocular and debonair" self, the newspapers reported. He pleaded not guilty, and new bail was set at $7,500.

In March 1908, Flora Whiston, one of the youths, appeared in court and denied the charges she made against the actor to the grand jury. She was swiftly arrested for perjury. The girl created a sensation in court by denying the actor had harmed her and accusing a child abuse investigator of inducing her to make the allegation. Whiston stated she was threatened with removal from her mother if she did not comply with testifying that

Hitchcock had sexually abused her. Based on this turn, the court dismissed the charges against Hitchcock on the Hagen case but retained the charges related to the Voeck case.

In June 1908, Hitchcock took the stand in his own defense. He painted a picture of the girls lurking about his property, pestering him at the stage door with requests for complimentary theater tickets and spreading lurid rumors.

Hitchcock claimed Helen von Hagen and another girl had waited for him outside the Garden Theatre and asked him for a ride home. He agreed, contingent on the consent of their mothers. After returning inside the theater, he came out again and found the girls inside his automobile, waving goodbye in the direction of the nearby Hagen residence. The actor first accompanied the girls on a ferry to Great Neck and then provided them with a meal and drove them to Long Island City.

Later, while on his boat on his private wharf, the actor testified, he observed the girls running from his property. Once Hitchcock returned to his home, his valet informed him that he found the girls inside the house and drove them away. Later that evening, Hitchcock and his valet observed the girls back on the property loitering on the front lawn. Hitchcock testified that he approached the girls, who admitted their mothers were not aware that they had returned to his property. Since it was late in the evening, Hitchcock allowed the girls to spend the night in one of the many guest suites in his mansion. The next morning, after the servants served the girls breakfast, Hitchcock drove them to the depot.

According to Hitchcock's testimony, Elsie Voecks later sought him out. The teen lamented that her mother had scolded her for staying out overnight and asked the actor to speak to her mother about the situation. The actor agreed. Shortly thereafter, at the Lambs Club, where Hitchcock and Thomas Meighan were members, the two girls came to speak with him again.

Hitchcock's valet testified that the actor gave Helena and Elsie a ride home but found them sitting on some steps inside the home the following Sunday. The girls were sent home again, but they returned to Hitchcock's porch. So, the actor took them in, gave them breakfast the following morning and sent them home. The valet also testified that he was present with Hitchcock—at the actor's request for his own protection—when the actor later confronted the girls in the city about the accusations circulating about him and William Astor Chanler. The girls denied making any accusations about the men. In testimony that benefitted the actor's defense, Helena's mother asserted her daughter had denied to her any wrongdoing by Hitchcock and Chanler.

At 2:50 a.m., on June 11, 1908, the jury returned to the courtroom following ninety minutes of deliberation. Having spent the previous night in jail, where the other inmates pressured him to perform songs from his famous musical reviews, Hitchcock stood to face the jury. His loyal wife, Flora, leaned forward to hear the verdict. It was like a scene out of the stage dramas in which the couple performed.

As the verdict was read, acquitting Hitchcock, Flora gasped with excitement and then sank in her chair while emitting a little cry. Friends and colleagues who had anxiously waited in court for the announcement of the verdict crowded around the actor. Raymond Hitchcock's name was cleared, and he was a free man.

What was public opinion of Hitchcock after this scandal? In October 1909, the actor received the loudest applause received by a thespian that season for his return to New York after a triumphant world tour.

The drama continued.

The Hitchcocks' House Fire

On the last day of August 1909, less than two months after the acquittal, a morning fire leveled the Hitchcocks' home while the couple was in Cleveland performing in the opening of George M. Hogan's musical *The Man Who Owned Broadway*.

A Swedish maid jumped from a third-floor window, surviving with a broken ankle, and millionaire neighbors, including William Astor Chanler, tried to use a garden hose to enter the home and rescue from the blaze valuable property, including oil paintings, tapestries and rare heirlooms, such as a century-old clock. They could not reach the mahogany bureau containing Flora's diamonds, which she left at home during her theatrical tour. Flora's mother, sister and cousin also survived the fire. According to newspapers, Flora fainted upon hearing about the destruction of her summer home.

In 1910, the couple built an exquisite three-story Colonial residence at 22 Sunset Road in Kings Point in the Great Neck area on the North Shore of Long Island. Boasting breathtaking panoramic water views of the Throgs Neck Bridge, Kings Point Lighthouse and the Manhattan skyline, the five-thousand-square-foot, six-bedroom, three-and-a-half-bath mansion featured stucco and slate, third-story dormers, wrought iron details and floor-to-ceiling windows that overlooked Long Island Sound. The one acre of property, with gardens designed by Addison Cairns Mizner, contained a private dock and a pathway to a private sandy beach with direct water access. In 2023, the Hitchcocks' former estate was listed for sale by Sotheby's International Realty for $6 million.

The drama continued.

Marital Separation

In 1912, Flora and Raymond separated and reconciled in dramatic fashion, all covered in detail by newspapers. When Flora sailed for Europe in July, there were reports of a quarrel at the dock in which Raymond attempted to obtain her signature on documents related to the sale of cattle on their farm. Whispers of infidelity on the part of Flora swept the theatrical society. Newspapers reported on an allegation that a fellow passenger by the name of "Charlie" was the cause of the commotion. Raymond set the record straight by explaining the man in question was Flora's cousin and in no way the cause of any serious quarrel.

Flora hurried home because she saw a personal advertisement in a French newspaper that reported her brother was seriously ill in Great Neck, Long Island. However, this was a ruse devised by Hitchcock to lure her home.

Sailing from Europe to New York under her maiden name and accompanied by members of her family, Flora faced reporters and cameramen with a "bewitching smile." "My husband and I have agreed to separate," she announced. "Financially, domestically and artistically."

"I have lived with him for seven years," Flora said. "That's long enough, don't you think? Certainly, it's longer than women generally live with actor husbands."

"The separation is complete and forever," she asserted.

Well, not completely—or forever.

Even the press at the time doubted this was the end of the marriage. "Those who remember how Flora Zabelle stood by Hitchcock when he was arrested on the charge of being implicated with young girls in New York," reported the press, "believe that the Hitchcocks will yet get together."

So they did.

Success in the 1920s

Raymond and Flora headed west to Hollywood, where Raymond costarred in films with John Barrymore, Fatty Arbuckle, Mabel Normand and Mack Sennett. Raymond earned a weekly salary of $2,500 while Arbuckle and Normand earned $500 less, and the couple established a second residence in Beverly Hills. Flora appeared in the silent film *The Red Widow* (1916) opposite John Barrymore. Raymond had played Barrymore's role in the 1911 Broadway production of *The Red Widow*.

Hitchcock achieved greatness in his long-running revue *Hitchy-Koo*, produced from 1917 to 1920. Leasing the Forty-Fourth Street Theatre, the actor renamed the venue Raymond Hitchcock's Forty-Fourth Street Theatre and became the only actor-manager to appear in his own play on Broadway. After each performance, he usually rushed to the theater lobby to shake hands with members of the audience and ask, "How'd you like the show?"

In 1921, Hitchcock—now nationally known as Hitchy—headlined the Ziegfeld Follies with Fanny Brice and W.C. Fields. The show featured Hitchy's trademark tagline, "Sufferin' sassafrass!" This signature line was later used as Daffy Duck's and Sylvester's tagline in the Warner Brothers Studios animated cartoon film series. Its connection to the stage superstar has been long forgotten.

In 1925, Hitchcock appeared in a test sound-on-film process, in which he performed a famous sketch from *Hitchy-Koo* and featured prominently in film director John Ford's *Upstream* (1927). His later films included *Red Heads Preferred* (1926), *Everybody's Acting* (1926), *The Monkey Talks* (1927) and *The Tired Business Man* (1927).

By the mid-1920s, Flora and Raymond had visited New Port Richey, where Flora's brother-in-law, Earl Benham, purchased and sold property. Flora, now retired from stage and film, wintered in the city while her husband toured. On Christmas Day 1925, the *New Port Richey Press* reported that Raymond and Flora had returned to the city and said Flora would remain for the winter as a guest of the Manor Inn and Hotel near the Gulf of Mexico.

On January 20, 1926, Flora—reported in the press as Mrs. Raymond Hitchcock—and her sister, Mrs. Earl Benham, entertained a bridge game at the Hitchcock home on Dixie Boulevard. Their guests included friends from Great Neck: Mr. and Mrs. George Sims, Mr. and Mrs. Ernest Truex, Mr. and Mrs. Robert Montgomery, Mr. and Mrs. Ed Wynn and Raymond

Hitchcock and Zabelle stroll past the First State Bank on Main Street, New Port Richey. *West Pasco Historical Society.*

Hitchcock. Flora had been spending the winter in town while Raymond breezed through Tampa for three performances of his latest revue touring the nation.

On January 14, Flora attended the premiere of Raymond's show *Greenwich Village Follies* at the Victory Theatre on the corner of Tampa and Zack Streets in Tampa. At the finale, the actor was presented with a leather wallet that contained an honorary life membership card to the New Port Richey Golf and Country Club. In February, Flora hosted an event at Club Biarritz in Tampa Shores on the border of Oldsmar and Town 'N' Country. By summer, the *New Port Richey Press* reported, the couple had purchased a lot on the east side of the Pithlachascotee River.

On March 26, 1926, the *New Port Richey Press* published a photograph of Flora and Raymond standing in front of the First State Bank on the northwest corner of Main Street and Grand Boulevard. The same photograph was reprinted in 1927 with the caption "'[Hitchy]' Pays Off'—He is seen here in front of the First State Bank after drawing enough of the necessary to stuff the handbag of his lovely wife, Flora Zabelle Hitchcock, the other, and after all most important part of the picture."

In a staged photograph on the Jasmin Point Golf Course in New Port Richey, Flora points in the direction of the hole as Mary Sarazen—the wife of golfer Gene Sarazen—poses with a golf club in hand, about to make a hole in one. Both ladies are sporting cloche hats, ubiquitous fashion items of the 1920s.

In 1928, Hitchcock made his last major stage appearance playing Cupid in *Just Fancy* in Boston. Although he was advised by doctors to rest in the spring of 1929, Hitchcock appeared in *Your Uncle Dudley*. Critics lauded his performance as one of his best. However, after a few days, the declining actor was unable to perform and was hospitalized.

Hitchcock suffered a heart attack and remained in critical condition for several weeks before he was transferred to Kansas City for specialized treatment. Three weeks later, Hitchcock returned home to Flora in Beverly Hills. Due to a series of heart attacks and the primitive cardiac interventions of the era, doctors provided little hope for a resumption of the sixty-four-year-old actor's stage career.

On the evening of November 25, 1929, Raymond and Flora took a short drive to a drugstore and returned home in the automobile. As they reached the driveway shortly after midnight, Raymond gasped and fell onto Flora's shoulder. He died instantaneously.

Upon Hitchcock's death, newspapers published tributes from many in the theatrical community and eulogized Hitchcock as a beloved and preeminent comedian of his generation.

Raymond was interred alongside his parents in a family lot in Woodlawn, New York. His headstone reads simply, "Actor."

Flora's last appearance on Broadway took place in the musical *The Girl from Home* at the Globe Theatre in 1920. She subsequently retired from the stage and screen and joined Jacques Bodart Inc. as an interior furnishing designer and business partner. Flora likely found support in her sister's husband, who owned an elite haberdashery in Manhattan.

In 1931, Flora left retirement with media fanfare to portray Mrs. Van Allen in the Broadway production of *The Man on Stilts*. "My reason for wanting to return to the stage," Flora told columnist James Muir, "is chiefly that I sort of feel closer to my husband when I'm in the profession in which we went along together so long. He was always in the theatre and when I'm on stage he feels near."

Flora spent her last years living on Lexington Avenue in Manhattan. At age eighty-eight, on October 7, 1968, she died in Presbyterian Hospital in New York City, surviving her husband by thirty-seven years.

In the *Green Book* magazine in 1913, Flora wrote an essay titled "I Want to Be Understood":

> *How I did work and struggle for the recognition which I received. I had a fear of professional stagnation; would I continue in an indefinite, unestablished way or, worse still, fall back into oblivion? But I determined to apply myself as hard as I could, never for a moment to lose sight of my ambition's goal, that of creating leading parts in Broadway musical plays, and I have tenaciously held to that ambition, with as great a desire to-day, and indeed greater, to win the approval of the public.*

In telling the story of Flora and Raymond and their link to the Hacienda Hotel, they are rescued from oblivion.

15

EARL BENHAM AND
CHRISTINE MANGASARIAN

In December 1925, the press reported William Torbert's Cotee Realty Company sale of the firm's 2,200 feet of waterfront land in Bay Shore Estates to an unidentified buyer. The *New Port Richey Press* announced, "Details of this transaction when made public before the end of the month will be as interesting as any real estate news New Port Richey has had for many moons."

The mysterious purchaser was Earl Benham (1886–1976), an actor, songwriter and tailor to entertainers, who resided on Stoner Avenue in Great Neck, Long Island, with his wife, Christine, and their son, James.

Born in Brooklyn, New York, Benham began his theatrical career at the age of seventeen singing in minstrel shows and traveling with the Primrose Group and, later, the Cohan and Harris Minstrels, managed by producers George M. Cohan and Sam H. Harris.

Benham later he appeared in many Broadway musical comedies, including George M. Cohan's musical production of *The Little Millionaire* (1911); Ziegfeld's *Winsome Widow* (1911), with Leon Errol and Mae West; *Very Good Eddie* (1915), with Ernest Truex; Ed Wynn's *Carnival* (1919); and Raymond Hitchcock's *Hitchy-Koo* (1919).

In May 1915, Benham married Christine Mangasarian, who was born in Chicago in 1893. She was the sister of stage and screen actor Flora Zabelle, who was married to stage and screen comedian Raymond Hitchcock. The Hitchcocks also resided in Great Neck.

In 1914, Earl and Christine appeared in Cohan and Harris's widely successful musical-comedy *The Beauty Shop*, starring Raymond Hitchcock. It played for eighty-eight performances. The following year, the couple appeared in Cohan's vaudeville act *Give Us Your Kind Applause*. Christine had also appeared in the chorus of Cohan and Harris's musical *The Red Widow* (1911–12), starring Hitchcock.

Earl Benham and Christine Mangasarian. *West Pasco Historical Society.*

Earl Benham was a man of many creative talents. He composed music and wrote lyrics for several popular ballads of the World War I era, such as "Curly Locks," "When" and "Little Broken Toys."

In 1920, Benham went into business as a custom tailor for prominent theatrical entertainers. Benham and Company occupied exclusive shops on East Fifty-Third Street and Madison Avenue in Manhattan. The shop was often mentioned on *The Lucy and Desi Comedy Hour* (1957–60), a television sitcom starring Lucille Ball and Desi Arnaz, when the characters relocated from Manhattan to Connecticut, where the Benham resided at the time.

In 1913, Benham purchased land in New Port Richey from George R. Sims and later sold some of his property to screen megastar Thomas Meighan and his brother James. Benham owned waterfront property in Bay Shore Estates on Oyster Bayou with Gulf of Mexico access in New Port Richey and sold lots to his theatrical friends in New York. Henry Quist filled and beautified the property and designed sea walling for the tract.

Irving Berlin purchased a homesite from Benham that was reportedly "suited to the seclusion" needed for the composition of "ditties," according to the press. Orchestra leader Paul Whiteman also purchased land from Benham and became Berlin's neighbor. Benham also sold land to Blanche Ring, the wife of actor Charles Winninger and sister of Thomas Meighan's wife, Frances Ring.

The Benhams and their young son appeared in a photograph published in the *New Port Richey Press* on February 26, 1926. This photograph included Thomas and Frances Meighan, George and Marjorie Sims and Flora Zabelle Hitchcock.

When the Meighan Theatre opened in July 1926, Benham's congratulatory telegram was read at the opening gala.

"The Hacienda will make New Port Richey," Benham told the press in February 1927 while attending the hotel's grand opening during his weeklong visit to the city following a week in Havana, Cuba. "It's almost unbelievable what a difference a first-class hotel has made in the city. And the news about the new golf course is most encouraging. It's certainly good to get back to town, and our only regret is that the season for us this year will be brief."

Benham visited New Port Richey three times during 1927. Arriving in Jacksonville, the Benhams and their young son, Jimmie, motored to New Port Richey, where mother and son would reside for the winter. "They will build their New Port Richey home in the same neighborhood as Irving Berlin, Paul Whiteman, Sam H. Harris, and Joseph Santley [actor and singer]," announced the press.

During one of the Benhams' visits in 1927, the press praised Christine, whose popularity "was ineradicably established last winter." The couple was entertained by George and Marjorie Sims with tennis and tea; they also attended a card party hosted by Joseph Foley and a City Club banquet and sailed on the gulf in Warren E. Burns's yacht. Earl returned to New York, and Christine traveled to Palm Beach to visit theatrical producer Sam H. Harris and his wife.

It was during the winter of 1927–28 that Earl and Christine posed for two famous photographs on the north veranda of The Hacienda with George and Marjorie Sims, Gene and Mary Sarazen, Frances Meighan and a German Shepherd. The photograph, possibly taken by Thomas Meighan, was published in the *Tampa Tribune* in January 1928.

Benham's comings and goings were documented in the press. He registered at the Hacienda Hotel in 1928 and February 1931. "Mr. Benham was received with great joy by his many friends," asserted the *New Port Richey Press*. "Mr. Benham is a regular winter visitor and will be registered with his friends at the Hacienda Hotel, which is fast becoming the mecca for the town's growing list of celebrities."

During New Port Richey's decline in the early 1930s, the Benhams purchased a property at 194 Candlewood Hill Road in Higganum, Connecticut. Named Juniper Ridge, the estate contained fifty acres, two lakes, a dam and a waterfall surrounded by woodland. The couple gutted the interior of the main house and remodeled it as their country resort where they entertained show business greats.

In 1964, the Benhams sold the property to Mount Sacred Heart of Hamden, Connecticut, for the use of the Sisters of the Apostles of the Sacred Heart of Jesus as a place of spiritual renewal. Today, the property serves as a spirituality center for religious organizations, such as groups of priests and religious congregations.

In later years, Benham was president of the Percy Williams Home, a luxury facility in East Islip for the aged actors and a trustee of the Actors Fund of America.

Earl Benham died at his home in Northport, Long Island, on March 21, 1976, at the age of eighty-nine. He was survived by his son, James, two grandchildren and two great-grandchildren.

Christine is not mentioned in Earl's obituary. She had either predeceased him, or they divorced. In the 1940 census, she is listed at age forty-five and born in Illinois about 1895. Christine served as the vice-president of Twelfth Night Club, the oldest women's theatrical organization in America.

Earl and Christine's only son, James Armen Benham (1917–2020), who spent his youth in New Port Richey, died at the age of ninety-three in Norwalk, Connecticut. After graduating from Princeton in 1939, he served as an ensign aboard the USS *Farragut* when it was attacked at Pearl Harbor on December 7, 1941, and received the Bronze Star for his heroic act of guiding the frigate out of the harbor to safety that day.

In 1955, Benham joined the Ted Bates Advertising Agency, where he held the position of senior vice-president and director until his retirement in 1980. He then volunteered with the National Executive Service Corps and in other philanthropic endeavors. Having learned a few tips from Gene Sarazen while he spent time on Jasmin Point Golf Course in New Port Richey, James remained an avid golfer and a member of the Wee Burn Country Club in Darien, Connecticut.

A memorial in Earl Benham's honor stands on Bank Street on the east side of the Hacienda Hotel, a reminder of the creative and talented actor-composer-tailor and his family's participation in the early development of New Port Richey.

16

THE HACIENDA'S FAMOUS GUESTS

A photograph of the Hacienda Hotel in the *New Port Richey Press*, published on May 2, 1930, carried this caption:

> *The foyer of the Hacienda Hotel, which was the scene of many brilliant social affairs during the season, just closed. Here were assembled at various times some of the most famous living celebrities of stage and screen, including Thomas Meighan, Leon Errol, Madeline Cameron, Frances Ring, Flora Zabelle, and numerous others as well as such noted writers as Bob Davis, George Ade, Ring Lardner, Hal W. Lanigan and others. Gay parties from St. Petersburg, Tampa, Clearwater and other cities motored here to enjoy the delightful atmosphere of this "Bit of Old Spain Amid the Palms."*

The Hacienda Hotel register book was once equal to an autograph book, filled with the signatures of motion picture stars and literati of the early twentieth century.

ED WYNN, COMEDIAN

In 1968, George Reginald "Bunt" Sims II (1906–1989), known as Reginald, told the *Tampa Bay Times* that he recalled when comedian Ed Wynn "arrived to visit with my parents [George and Marjorie Sims] for three weeks and to rest up between schedules." Reginald's father, George, suggested Wynn take his boat to go fishing on the river, but the comedian confessed he couldn't even bait a hook. George arranged for a guide to accompany Wynn, and on the first day of fishing, he caught several trout. Wynn fished the remainder of his visit.

Abruptly, Wynn told George he had to return to New York to produce a play.

George Sims asked, "How in the world can you start production when you haven't yet written a play?"

"But I have written it," Wynn replied.

Ed Wynn (1886–1966) had completed an entire draft of a script while sitting in the boat waiting for the fish to bite. Reginald Sims believed the comedian had penned during the visit *The Perfect Fool*, which opened in Pittsburgh in 1921, but newspaper reporting of Wynn's production first arrived in New Port Richey in 1926.

According to the *Tampa Morning Tribune,* on November 12, 1926, Ed Wynn arrived in New Port Richey as a guest of George and Marjorie Sims "to write an original story for his comedy to be made next month by Famous Players."

"Everybody knows Ed Wynn is in town," *New Port Richey Press* announced with humorous inside knowledge on November 19. "But the *Press* refuses to discuss the matter. When the darn zany gets sense enough to stop catching cold on the Pithlachascotee River and sets himself down in front of a typewriter long enough to write the story he promised to write, he'll restore himself to good standing with this office. Nobody can tell the world about Ed Wynn as well as Ed Wynn can tell it himself."

The *Tampa Tribune* had announced Wynn's arrival in New Port Richey with Earl Benham on November 12. The comic was in town to write an original screenplay for his debut performance in a film to be produced by Famous Players. Wynn told the press he had known Sims and Benham for fifteen years in Great Neck and was a guest of George and Marjorie Sims for two weeks and planned to fish for trout.

Gossip maven Louella Parsons also mentioned Wynn's appearance in Florida in her nationally syndicated column, spotlighting the town to her readers: "Right now Mr. Wynn is in New Port Richey, Fla., basking in the sunshine and trying to think of a lot of new gags, while his friend Victor Heerman jots them down."

Wynn eventually made his big screen debut in Paramount's *Rubber Heels* (1927), directed by Victor Heerman.

According to the *New Port Richey Press*, during Wynn's visit in 1926, Warren E. Burns coordinated a "stag party" on his yacht, the *Lola Dean*, and hosted a fishing excursion for Wynn, Thomas Meighan, James Meighan, Earl Benham and George Sims. Because of Wynn's antics, the group returned without fish. According to Earl Benham, "The fishes laughed so frequently that they had no time to bite."

Wynn, who discovered his humor at an early age when he paraded in ladies' hats for comic relief, embarked upon an entertainment career in vaudeville in 1903 and starred in the *Ziegfeld Follies* beginning in 1914. In the subsequent decades, Wynn wrote, directed and produced many Broadway musical revues, including *Ed Wynn Carnival* (1920), *The Perfect Fool* (1921) and *The Laugh Parade* (1931). His schtick featured silly hats, costumes, props and a giggly, lisping voice originally developed for *The Perfect Fool*, an act that became his much-loved signature piece.

In *Hooray for What!* (1937), an antifascist, antiwar musical, Wynn starred as Chuckles, a mild-mannered chemist who accidentally invents a poisonous gas that could be used to take over the world. The protagonist sells his poisonous gas to the League of Nations Peace Conference in Geneva, where it turns into a love potion.

Wynn fought against being blacklisted after he joined a national actors strike in 1919 and infuriated his employers by resisting their court injunction to join an actors benefit show. That same year, Wynn began an active membership of the Lambs Club and was fellow Lamb Thomas Meighan's neighbor in Great Neck, Long Island, where George Sims also resided.

The comedian garnered a mass following when he reached North American audiences on the popular radio show *The Fire Chief* on Tuesday evenings between 1932 and 1935, sponsored by Texaco gasoline. His character's falsetto voice and playful puns amused millions of listeners.

On June 4, 1933, O.O. McIntyre's syndicated column reported a one-liner, "Ed Wynn owns a theater at New Port Richey, Fla.," in which the journalist likely referred to the Palms Theatre on Main Street. A 1937 article in the *St. Petersburg Evening Independent* mentioned Wynn also owning the Leeston-Smith building, which adjoined the Thomas Meghan Theatre on Boulevard in New Port Richey.

As a visual comic, Wynn transitioned to early live television on *The Ed Wynn Show* on CBS and received the first Emmy Award as the Most Outstanding Live Personality. Lucille Ball and Desi Arnaz appeared in an episode in 1949 before *I Love Lucy* debuted.

In the mid-1950s, while costarring with his son Keenan Wynn, Ed demonstrated dramatic talent on television in a live dramatic broadcast of Rod Steiger's teleplay *Requiem for a Heavyweight* on an episode of *Playhouse 90* on CBS.

Wynn's dramatic film roles included the owner of a Christian radio station in *The Great Man* (1956), for which he was nominated for a Golden Globe Award, and the Dutch dentist in *The Diary of Anne Frank* (1959), for which he was nominated for an Academy Award as Best Supporting Actor. In an unexpected casting, Wynn portrayed Aram, the elderly blind man, in director George Stevens's epic about Jesus of Nazareth, *The Greatest Story Ever Told* (1966).

Ed Wynn (1886–1966). *PICRYL public domain archive, Get Archive LLC (public domain).*

A versatile performer, Wynn alternated with comic roles, such as the fairy godfather in *Cinderfeller* (1960), the fire chief in *The Absent-Minded Professor* (1963) and Uncle Albert in *Mary Poppins* (1964).

When Ed Wynn died in 1966, comic Red Skelton, who was discovered by Wynn, stated, "His death is the first time he ever made anyone sad."

Wynn has often been credited with serving as the master of ceremonies at the grand opening gala of the Hacienda Hotel. Allegedly, the film and radio comic expressed his great pleasure of visiting "the most beautiful city imaginable."

CHARLOTTE GREENWOOD, ACTOR

On March 2, 1928, the *New Port Richey Press* reported that Charlotte Greenwood (1893–1978), a star of vaudeville, Broadway and film, had secured a riverfront lot along Dixie Boulevard and planned to build a mansion like that of Thomas Meighan, her costar in *Cheaters at Play* (1932). At five feet, ten inches tall and remarkably double-jointed, Greenwood was famous for her ability to lift her leg above her head at a ninety-degree angle to her body.

Charlotte Greenwood (1890–1977). *PICRYL public domain archive, Get Archive LLC (public domain).*

During World War II, Greenwood portrayed wise-cracking, high-kicking roles in Technicolor musicals, such as *Down Argentine Way* (1940), with Carmen Miranda; *Tall, Dark and Handsome* (1941); *Moon Over Miami* (1941), with Don Ameche and Betty Grable; *Springtime in the Rockies* (1942), with Betty Grable and Cesar Romero; and *The Gang's All Here* (1943). In the latter, a middle-aged Greenwood performs an acrobatic jitterbug with a youthful male dance partner.

The role of Aunt Eller in the film adaptation of Rodgers and Hammerstein's *Oklahoma!* (1955), created with her in mind for the stage production in 1943, became Greenwood's sobriquet.

Frank Case, Hotelier

Frank Case (1872–1946) was an American hotelier and author who owned and managed the Algonquin Hotel on Forty-Fourth Street in New York during the heyday of the Algonquin Round Table. The wedding of George Reginald Sims's son Reginald "Bunt" Sims was held at the landmark hotel in 1937.

The Algonquin Round Table comprised Manhattan writers, critics, actors and wits. Dubbed the "Vicious Circle," they met at the hotel for lunch each day between 1919 and 1929, and there, they engaged in wisecracks, wordplay and witticisms, which members dispersed to readers of their syndicated newspaper columns. The group's membership included Dorothy Parker, Robert Benchley, Alexander Woollcott, Franklin P. Adams, Edner Ferber, Heywood Broun, George S. Kaufman and Robert E. Sherwood.

Employed by the hotel at the time of its opening in 1902, Case took over the lease in 1907 and became its manager, eventually buying the hotel in 1927 for $1 million. He remained the owner and manager of the Algonquin until his death in 1946.

Frank Case (1872–
1946) at far right.
*PICRYL public domain
archive, Get Archive LLC
(public domain).*

In New York, Case socialized with Flora Zabelle and Thomas Meighan. In 1927, Case was photographed with Flora Zabelle, who frequented the Algonquin Hotel with her husband, Raymond Hitchcock. The actors eventually coaxed him to New Port Richey, where the hotelier registered at The Hacienda during the winters of 1928 and 1934. During his second documented visit, Case caught a ten-pound redfish in the Pithlachascotee River, according to the *New Port Richey Press*, after expertly angling it for twenty minutes.

RING LARDNER, WRITER

Ringgold "Ring" Wilmer Lardner (1885–1933) was a gifted satirist who began his career as a journalist in 1905 as a reporter for the *South Bend Times* in Indiana. He transitioned to newspapers in Chicago, where he established a reputation as a sportswriter specializing in baseball stories.

In 1913, Lardner accepted a position with the *Chicago Tribune* as a columnist who wrote the widely popular daily syndicated "In the Wake of the News," which expanded his repertoire in over 1,600 columns. He also penned a humorous weekly column for the *Bell Syndicate* from 1919 to 1927. On assignment from *Collier's* magazine in 1918, Lardner headed off to France to cover World War I.

Lardner influenced American writing arguably greater than any other twentieth-century writer before the ascent of Ernest Hemingway. His crisp, sardonic, satirical style employed vernacular language and slang representative of the era. As a student, Hemingway used the pseudonym "Ring Lardner Jr." in several articles parodying Lardner's style published in the Oak Park High School newspaper in Illinois.

While writing his column, Lardner published fiction and sold baseball stories to the *Saturday Evening Post*. He had achieved success with stories featuring the character Jack Keefe, a comic minor-league pitcher, and some of these stories were collected in *You Know Me Al* (1916).

Lardner attracted critical accolades with his collection *How to Write Short Stories* (1924) and *The Love Nest and Other Stories* (1926), with a notable title story adapted by playwright Robert E. Sherwood in 1927.

Exploring subjects such as marriage and the theater, Lardner collaborated with George M. Cohan on *Elmer the Great* (1928) and with George S. Kaufman on *June Moon* (1929), a Broadway musical comedy for which he also wrote songs. Lardner also penned lyrics and comic sketches for the *Ziegfeld Follies*, including one that featured Will Rogers as a veteran pitcher.

In 1921, Lardner, his wife, Ellis, and their four sons relocated to Great Neck, Long Island, where, between 1922 and 1924, the writer—then in his late thirties—befriended his neighbor F. Scott Fitzgerald (1896–1940), who was then in his mid-twenties. The only things they had in common were their genius, alcohol and the compatibility of their wives. Zelda Fitzgerald did not always approve of Scott's friends, but she adored Lardner.

According to Matthew J. Bruccoli, a preeminent expert on F. Scott Fitzgerald, Lardner engaged in an elaborate mock courtship of Zelda. In a poem he sent Zelda, he poked fun at Scott in the fourth line:

> *Of all the girls for whom I care,*
> *And there are quite a number,*
> *None can compare with Zelda Sayre,*
> *Now wedded to a plumber.*

In his fourth and final novel, *Tender Is the Night*, released in 1934, Fitzgerald patterned the character Abe North, an alcoholic composer murdered in a New York speakeasy, after Ring Lardner.

Lardner transcended to screenwriting with *The New Klondike* (1926), starring Thomas Meighan, his friend and neighbor in Great Neck, Long Island; it was the first film shown at the opening of the Meighan Theatre in New Port Richey. Paramount Pictures produced a film adaptation of Larner's *Elmer the Great*, titled *Fast Company* (1929), followed by First National Pictures' adaptation, titled *Elmer the Great* (1933), starring Joe E. Brown.

Ring Lardner (1885–1933, *second from right*). *Left to right*: President Warren G. Harding, Grantland D. Rice, Lardner, Secretary of State Henry P. Fletcher. *PICRYL public domain archive, Get Archive LLC (public domain)*.

The material was later adapted into the film *The Cowboy Quarterback* (1939), starring Bert Wheeler and William Demarest.

In February 1926, a photograph of Lardner in a boat on the Cotee River appeared on the front page of the *New Port Richey Press* when he and fellow sportswriter Grantland Rice, whom Lardner called "Granny," were part of a fishing party. The writers were guests of Christine Benham, the wife of Earl Benham, and Flora Zabelle, the wife of Raymond Hitchcock, who owned property near Lardner in Great Neck.

The witty satirist told reporters that next time, he planned to bring an assortment of bait for the un-hungry fish and "scatter printed menus on the waters of the river to be distributed by the tidal process before he makes his first cast." Lardner mentioned the city in his column in April 1926.

After contracting tuberculosis, Lardner was frequently hospitalized in his last seven years.

When Lardner died in 1933 at the age of forty-eight, F. Scott Fitzgerald wrote an elegy, "Ring," for the *New Republic*, in which he lamented, "One wishes that Ring had written down a larger portion of what was in his mind and heart. It would have saved him longer for us, and that in itself would be something."

George Ade, Writer

The *Chicago Tribune* described George Ade (1866–1944), a playwright and humorist from Indiana, as a "two-fisted drinker" and "one of the most gregarious men who ever lived." A lifelong bachelor, Ade enjoyed a good time, and after World War I, he turned his attention to experiencing good times.

Following his graduation from Purdue University, Ade was on the staff of the *Chicago Record* from 1890 to 1900. The characters Ade introduced in his widely acclaimed editorial column, "Stories of the Streets and of the Town," became the subjects of his early books *Artie* (1896), *Pink Marsh* (1897) and *Doc Horne* (1899).

Ade achieved critical recognition for his *Fables in Slang* (1899), a bestseller that inspired a weekly syndicated fable and a series of books of fables that contain the wisdom accumulated by the narrative of a country boy in the city. Between 1914 and 1917, the Essenay Film Company adapted over sixty of Ade's fables into ten-minute short films.

In 1902, Ade penned an opera, *The Sultan of Sulu*, followed by successful stage comedies, such as *The County Chairman* (1903) and *The College Widow* (1904). Famous Players–Lasky Corporation adapted *The County Chairman* into a film in 1914.

Ade wrote screenplays for three motion pictures starring Thomas Meighan and distributed by Paramount Pictures: *Our Leading Citizen* (1922), *Back Home and Broke* (1922) and *Woman-Proof* (1923).

During the waning Prohibition era, Ade published *The Old Time Saloon* (1931), an amusing exercise in nostalgia that reminded dry readers of the pleasures of alcohol and socializing in saloons.

In 1927, George Ade's endorsement of vacationing in Florida appeared in an advertisement promoting the opening of the Hacienda Hotel, published in the *New Port Richey Press* on January 21, 1927. "Florida from October to May, Suggests George Ade," proclaimed the headline. "Those who have lived in New Port Richey know that Mr. Ade is right. New Port Richey's climate is equable and pleasant for twelve months not eight months of the year. Our new hotel, The Hacienda, will be ready to accommodate guests."

Ade visited New Port Richey in 1930, according to the *New Port Richey Press*, which described the writer in a 1931 edition as a "staunch supporter of Florida and a regular visitor."

On January 23, 1931, the *New Port Richey Press* announced the writer's expected arrival two days later: "George Ade Arrives in This Town, Famous Writer Here to Visit His Friend Thomas Meighan." The article reported Ade "will be domiciled in an especially appointed suite of rooms at the Hotel Hacienda" and will "play some golf with his old friend" Meighan on the Jasmin Point Golf Course.

George Ade (1866–1944). *PICRYL public domain archive, Get Archive LLC (public domain).*

On February 18, 1932, the *Miami News* announced Thomas Meighan had arrived the previous day from his residence in New Port Richey and registered at the King Cole Hotel. The article also mentioned that George Ade, having visited the west coast of Florida, arrived with Meighan and registered at the same hotel. Two weeks prior, the *St. Petersburg Times* reported that Ade had suffered a "nervous breakdown" while a guest at the Belleair Biltmore Hotel and was hospitalized in Clearwater.

The West Pasco Historical Society's archive contains a photograph of George Ade with Thomas Meighan and Frank Finnegan.

DOROTHY DALTON, ACTOR

On January 28, 1928, the *Tampa Daily Times* published under the headline "Here Are the Reasons for Popularity in New Port Richey" a photograph of Dorothy Dalton, with the wife of Sam H. Harris, standing in front of the Hacienda Hotel holding a large fish from a hook.

Dorothy Dalton (1893–1972) was a silent film actor and stage personality who ascended from working at a stock company to a motion picture career. Beginning in 1910, Dalton was a player in stock companies in Chicago and Holyoke, Massachusetts. She joined the Keith-Albee-Orpheum Corporation's vaudeville circuits and quickly transitioned to the Triangle Film Corporation, where she debuted in *Pierre of the Plains* (1914), costarring Edgar Selwyn, followed by a leading role in *Across the Pacific* that same year. Dalton appeared with William S. Hart in *The Disciple* (1915), a redemption-themed western.

Dalton's brief Broadway career included a performance as Chrysis in *Aphrodite* (1919–20).

Dalton signed with Thomas Harper Ince Studios from 1919 until director Ince's death in 1924. During this period, Dalton costarred with William Conklin in *The Price Mark* (1917) and *Love Letters* (1917) and with H.B. Warner in *The Vagabond Prince* (1916) and *The Flame of the Yukon* (1917). She

Dorothy Dalton (1893–1972). *PICRYL public domain archive, Get Archive LLC (public domain).*

also appeared with Rudolph Valentino in *Moran of the Lady Letty* (1922), distributed by Paramount Pictures.

In 1924, Dalton married theatrical producer Arthur Hammerstein, the uncle of Oscar Hammerstein II, the famous lyricist and son of Oscar Hammerstein I. Following the marriage, she retired from film.

In 1943, Dalton and Hammerstein purchased the Gieseke Farm in Hoffman Estates in the Chicago suburbs and raised pure-blooded and registered Duroc Jersey hogs and Holstein dairy cattle. The couple jokingly called the farm "Headacres."

LEON ERROL, ACTOR

According to the *New Port Richey Press*, Leon Errol and his wife, actor Stella Chatelaine, spent Christmas 1929 with Thomas Meighan and his wife, Frances, at their New Port Richey mansion and the Hacienda Hotel. On January 1, 1930, the *Tampa Times* reported Meighan made a reservation for ten among three hundred revelers to celebrate New Year's Eve and the start of a new decade at the Davis Island Country Club in Tampa; the Meighan party included Errol and Chatelaine and Gene and Mary Sarazen (see chapter 16).

The *New Port Richey Press* also reported in January 1930 that George and Marjorie Sims entertained at their home adjacent to Sims Park the Errols, the Meighans, the Sarazens and actor Madeline Cameron, unaccompanied by her husband, actor William Gaxton.

Born in Australia, Leon Errol (1881–1951) began performing in the circus, light operas and Shakespearean plays before immigrating to the United States in 1904 with his dance partner, Stella Chatelaine (1886–1946).

Performing cockney songs and eccentric dances in saloons, Errol partnered with Pete Gerald in "Gerald and Errol," a traveling vaudeville act involving German and Irish dialect comedy, a ragtime piano, burlesque boxing and a trained bulldog named Buck.

Leon Errol and Stella Chatelaine were married in 1906 and took their burlesque comedy revue to New York. Soon, Florenz Ziegfeld arranged for Errol's Broadway debut in *The Winsome Widow*, costarring Earl Benham (see chapter 18), and then cast him and Chatelaine in the *Ziegfeld Follies* (1911–15). Errol coproduced and performed in two revues of *Hitchy-Koo*, a series of musical revues inspired by a song staged on Broadway from 1917 to 1920 and a tour in 1922, produced by and starring Raymond Hitchcock (see chapter 17).

Leon Errol (1881–1951). *PICRYL public domain archive, Get Archive LLC (public domain).*

Transitioning to motion pictures in 1925 and signing with RKO Radio Pictures in 1930, Errol achieved success in long-running series of short comic films for RKO Radio Pictures from 1934 until his death in 1951. In 1939, Errol costarred with Lupe Vélez (1908–1944) in *The Girl from Mexico*. The B film's success led to RKP reteaming the costars in a sequel, *The Mexican Spitfire* (1940), and a series of Mexican Spitfire films, eight in total.

Aside from Errol's link to New Port Richey's own Thomas Meighan, George Sims, Earl Benham and Raymond Hitchcock, the *New Port Richey Press* reported that the actor "has been for some time an owner of New Port Richey property, purchased through James Meighan; it is not known at this time whether the star plans to build."

WALTER DONALDSON, COMPOSER AND SONGWRITER

On January 16, 1931, *New Port Richey Press* announced, "Eminent Composer Is Visitor, Walter Donaldson Now Registered at the Hacienda Hotel."

"To add to his accomplishments, Donaldson is a pianist of marvelous ability and an excellent golfer," the newspaper gushed. "He will spend some little time in New Port Richey to be near his friend, Thomas Meighan, and will play golf with Gene Sarazen, Al Ciuci, and Henry Ciuci. Although these gentlemen are among the best golf pros in the country, all agree they will have to be at the top of their game to beat Walter Donaldson." Donaldson's extended visit included his participation in a festive bridge party held at The Hacienda in early February, attended by the Meighans, Sarazens and married film stars Madeline Cameron and William Gaxton.

Considered one of the most famous songwriters of the Jazz Age, Walter Donaldson (1893–1947) was born in Brooklyn, New York, and began his professional music career as a staff pianist in Tin Pan Alley. He composed a litany of hit songs in the 1910s to the 1940s that have become standards and form part of the Great American Songbook.

Donalson's first published ragtime song, "Back Home in Tennessee," was released in 1915, but his first hit, "The Daughter of Rosie O'Grady," came the following year. He continued composing throughout his enlistment in the army during World War I and frequently entertained troops. After Donaldson joined composer Irving Berlin's publishing firm, his songs were regularly featured in vaudeville shows before the advent of radio. Al Jolson introduced "My Mammy" in the Broadway show *Sinbad* (1918), making the song Donaldson's first success on the Great White Way.

The period between 1925 and 1928, leading up to Donaldson's visit to the Hacienda Hotel, was the composer's most productive and lucrative era.

Donaldson made hundreds of compositions, including many of the legendary songs of the 1910s and 1920s: "My Little Bimbo Down on the Bamboo Isle," "My Mammy," "My Buddy," "Carolina in the Morning," "(What Can I Say) After I Say I'm Sorry," "My Blue Heaven," "That Certain Party," "Don't Be Angry," "He's the Last Word," "Changes" and "Thinking Of You." Many of his song titles included the word *baby*, the era's vernacular word for a romantic partner: "Yes Sir, That's My Baby," "I Wonder Where My Baby Is Tonight," "Because My Baby Don't Mean Maybe Now," "There Ain't No Maybe in My Baby's Eyes" and "Oh, Baby!"

The great lyricist Gus Kahn wrote the words for many of Donaldson's most popular compositions. Kahn penned the lyrics to numerous classic hits, including "Ain't We Got Fun," "Toot, Toot, Tootsie (Goodbye)," "It Had to Be You" and "Dream a Little Dream of Me."

In 1928, Donaldson formed his own music publishing firm, Donaldson, Douglas and Gumble, with partners Walter Douglas and Mose Gumble. That same year, he and Gus Kahn collaborated in writing the score for the successful *Ziegfeld Follies* show *Whoopee*, featuring the classics "Makin' Whoopee," sung by Eddie Cantor, and "Love Me or Leave Me," sung by Ruth Etting. For Samuel Goldwyn's film adaptation of the stage show, Donaldson and Kahn wrote yet another classic, "My Baby Just Cares for Me."

Prolific until his death, Donaldson wrote many of the world's best-loved standards and was nominated for an Academy Award for the song "Did I Remember" from the film *Suzy* (1936), starring Jean Harlow and Cary Grant.

During World War II, Donaldson entertained in the USO, the Hollywood Canteen and various Allied Resistance Benefits.

Bob Langford, Musician and Music Producer

Bob Langford, born in 1942, is a music legend whose humility underscored his immense talent, professional successes and service to New Port Richey. Bob was the lead singer in his band the Intruders, the opening act for the Rolling Stones when they performed at Jack Russell Stadium in Clearwater. The Intruders performed longer than the headlining act, as law enforcement had to end the concert early due to the audience's disruptive behavior. Incidentally, the Rolling Stones reportedly completed writing "Satisfaction" at the Fort Harrison Hotel during this visit to Clearwater in May 1965, shortly before they recorded it a few days later in Los Angeles.

By 1969, Langford had become an integral part of the exploding Atlanta recording industry managing, promoting and recording music. With a specialty in sound engineering, Langford recorded with Blood, Sweat & Tears; Deep Purple; Jerry Lee Lewis; the Classic IV; Billy Joe Royal; Joe South; and the Atlanta Rhythm Section. Langford is renowned for mixing southern rock band Lynyrd Skynyrd's emotionally and culturally affecting nine-minute song "Free Bird" for their 1973 debut album. At first, the band's front man, Ronnie Van Zant, and the other band members objected to Langford's mixing of between eight and eleven guitar tracks into the two tracks that comprised the song's four-minute guitar solo, chiefly because they could never play live the way it was recorded. Finally, producer Al Kooper approved the track, knowing the potential for a hit release after first hearing it. The rest is history. Langford also recorded half of the band's follow-up album, *Second Helping*, including its mega-hit rock anthem, "Sweet Home Alabama."

Langford was also responsible for Lynyrd Skynyrd's idiosyncratically spelled name—mockingly named after a former high school gym coach who enforced the dress code's prohibition of long hair and sideburns—by substituting Ys for vowels.

Born and raised in Louisville, Kentucky, Langford sang at Durrett High School in the late 1950s, and he also performed in bands and recorded songs that were played on the radio. After his graduation in 1960, he relocated with his mother and stepfather, Joe and Lillian Peak, to Gulf Harbors, a waterfront community then called Flor-a-Mar, in New Port Richey. Joe was a sergeant in the New Port Richey Police Department, and Lillian owned Lillian's Beauty Salon.

In 1964, Langford's next group, the Capris, performed in Cocoa Beach to audiences that often included astronauts from NASA at Cape Canaveral, where launching rockets often interrupted the music. Mike Olson, later a Pasco tax collector, played the saxophone, and Bertie Higgins, later famous for his 1982 hit "Key Largo," was a drummer.

Langford's younger brother, Lanny, played football and graduated from Gulf High School in 1963. As the lead singer of the Roemans, a group also that also featured Bertie Higgins, Lanny opened for the Animals at Fort Homer Hesterly Armory in Tampa in 1965. Considered New Port Richey's version of the Beatles, the Roemans toured England, where they recorded. After meeting John, Paul, George and Ringo, the Roemans employed the Fab Four's tailor to design their performing suits.

In 1966, Bob Langford left New Port Richey to become an integral part of Atlanta's music scene, where he befriended then-senator Julian Bond and then-mayor Andrew Young. Langford participated in civil rights marches and helped broadcast speeches by Dr. Martin Luther King. Although he admired John F. Kennedy and became an activist, Langford avoided politics.

Meanwhile, Lanny became known as the rock star who became a New Port Richey police officer alongside his stepfather. Three months after becoming a Tarpon Springs police officer in 1969, Lanny was tragically killed while on duty when a driver who was passing on a hill on Tarpon Avenue collided head-on with his police cruiser.

Still reeling from his younger brother's death, Langford returned to New Port Richey with his wife in 1998. He attended city council meetings and served on the Tampa Bay Regional Planning Council, the board of directors of the Suncoast League of Cities, Leadership Florida, the West Pasco Chamber of Commerce, the Chasco Fiesta Entertainment Committee and numerous other local organizations.

Langford served New Port Richey as chairman of the City Charter and Ordinance Review Board in 1999–2000 and currently serves as the chairman of the City Historical Preservation Board. He refurbished, restored and preserved the city's historic fire department map, currently displayed in Ordinance One Brewery on Main Street.

No longer shying away from politics, Langford was elected deputy mayor in 2003, when he ousted an incumbent. In 2006, he narrowly lost the mayoral election by thirty-three votes to the incumbent.

As a founding member of Friends of The Hacienda, he served as the group's president, establishing, leading and accomplishing goals to bring to fruition the vision city leaders and the hotel's developer upheld for the landmark. He championed the commemorative engraved brick path that leads from The Hacienda to Sims Park, where he also placed brass benches. By the time of his resignation as president, Langford had taken the group from being $60 in debt to a healthy $60,000 account balance.

Bob Langford. *West Pasco Historical Society*.

Langford continues to produce music and owns a recording studio and a recording label. As an inventor and electronics wizard, he patented an audio signal processing system in 1977.

Widowed, Langford reconnected with his brother's classmate Ann Rusaw while she was visiting New Port Richey for her Gulf High School class of 1963 reunion, and the couple later married. They remain active in the West Pasco Historical Society and are part of the leadership of community events and nonprofit organizations that promote the city and preserve its heritage.

AL CAPONE, GANGSTER

Despite local lore, there is no evidence that Al Capone was a guest of the Hacienda Hotel or the Moon Lake Casino and Dude Ranch, as the latter's historical marker implied. In another chapter, we will explore the truth behind the legend of The Hacienda's "bordello rooms," often attributed to the notorious gangster. But what's the truth about Capone's link to the Suncoast?

On February 10, 1931, the *St. Petersburg Times* reported on its front page, "Al Capone Pays Visit to the City." The article detailed his moves:

Al "Scarface" Capone, reputed king of Chicago's gangland, paid a visit to Pinellas County Monday, spending a few hours in St. Petersburg and later motoring to Tarpon Springs, where he spent considerable time looking over the sponge industry. Capone, with a party of five, including one woman, was seen here by several persons.

Later that afternoon, a large crowd gathered at the Sponge Exchange in Tarpon Springs to see the famous baronial head of the beer racket. Capone's business on Florida's west coast could not be ascertained, but there was plenty of speculation. Shortly thereafter, Capone purchased a 14-room estate on Palm Island, near Miami, from August Anheuser Busch, the beer magnate.

When the Moon Lake Casino and Dude Ranch opened in 1937, Capone had already served five of a total of seven years in prison. In 1931, the gangster was tried, found guilty, fined and sentenced to eleven years in prison.

In 1939, suffering from the late stages of syphilis, Capone was released and entered a Baltimore hospital, where he remained for three years in a state of dementia caused by the venereal disease. Later, Capone retired to his estate on Palm Island, where he died in 1947.

No documentation exists confirming Capone ever made a visit to New Port Richey. In a 1941 deposition, Capone's wife, Mae, stated he arrived in St. Petersburg for a "short visit…fourteen or fifteen years ago [1926 or 27]." The gangster's link to the Hacienda Hotel is largely apocryphal, similar to Gloria Swanson's. However, you might want to avoid correcting the local tour guides.

17

THE DECLINE

Although many of the local historic mansions built by former guests of the Hacienda Hotel and those luminary guests of the early twentieth century have since faded away, the hotel stands in the twenty-first century as an enduring symbol of New Port Richey's golden era and a beacon for its present and future.

Unfortunately, few remember the actor who wintered in New Port Richey and put the city on the map. Thomas Meighan returned to New York one spring and never returned. From the time he first visited and until his death, Meighan completed fifteen films. In 1934, the actor was diagnosed with cancer. The following year, he underwent surgery at Doctors Hospital in Manhattan.

On March 15, 1935, the *New Port Richey Press* reported on Meighan's last visit to the city:

> *Thomas Meighan, well known screen star who maintains a palatial residence in New Port Richey, arrived in the city Wednesday with Mrs. Meighan to spend some time in this locality. The Meighans had been visiting in Miami prior to coming back to the West Coast. They traveled by plane as far as Clearwater, being met there by Geo. R. Sims and escorted to New Port Richey.*

On the evening of July 8, 1936, Meighan succumbed to his illness shortly after lapsing into a coma at the age of fifty-seven. The actor died at home on Grenwolde Drive at King's Point in Great Neck, Long Island. The actor was surrounded by his wife, Frances; brother James E. Meighan; sister May Meighan; and Stella Chatelaine, the wife of comedian Leon Errol. The actor was also survived by two other brothers, John A. Meighan and William J. Meighan, and another sister, Mrs. M.C. Schneider.

Meighan was originally buried at Calvary Cemetery in Queens, New York, but the following year, his remains were relocated to a family plot at Saint Mary's Cemetery in the actor's hometown of Pittsburgh, according to his wishes.

On October 30, 1936, the *Dade City Banner* reported that Meighan's estate was sold to Irving R. Allen of Chicago. The deed, signed by Frances Ring Meighan and Arthur M. Munn, executors of the estate, denoted a cash price of $30,000. Munn operated the Chasco Inn on Main Street.

In 1939, the former Meighan estate was sold to Addison Q. Miller of St. Paul, Minnesota, a contractor and builder of railroads, dams, war projects and public structures. Unmarried, Miller wintered in the mansion and later purchased the Meighan Theatre. He died in 1944.

Later, V.N. Clark Jr. and his wife, Celida, purchased the former Meighan estate. Clark had developed Hudson Beach Estates, and Celida was a real estate broker specializing in waterfront properties.

In the fall of 1960, Meighan's Casa Francesca at Jasmin Point was scheduled for demolition when the property was subdivided into five lots and auctioned. No one mentioned the option of preservation. However, in mid-century Pasco County, the maintenance of the estate may have been unaffordable to most.

The contents of the mansion were offered up at an estate sale announced in the *Tampa Tribune*, including "unusual furniture," custom loomed broadlooms, crystal chandeliers, wrought iron furniture and railings, hand-painted tiles, Chinese and Turkestan rugs and a museum-quality Ming incense burner. According to Lucy O'Brien, the mansion's contents went to auction, and prospective buyers and curiosity seekers roamed amid the fallen plaster and exhausted Oriental rugs. Strolling through the romantic entrances, through which one master bedroom led to another, and gazing at the immensity of closets and dressing rooms, one hardly knew whether to celebrate or mourn the loss of the structure.

Three of the five lots that once belonged to the famous film star were sold immediately, one for just under $5,000 and two for just over $5,000. Bids on the other two, including one that contained the actor's bathhouse and enormous swimming pool, did not result in successful hammer bids.

New modern homes sprang up on the site of the old mansion, and except for large magnolias and palms and a concrete fence, the only relics of the Meighan estate were the old swimming pool and solarium.

Thomas Meighan's friend and golf legend Gene Sarazen lived the last years of his life on Marco Island, Florida. His wife of sixty-two years, Mary Catherine, died in 1986. When Sarazen died at the age of ninety-seven in 1999, he was survived by a daughter, Mary Ann Sarazen, of Marco Island; a son, Gene Sarazen Jr., of Delray Beach; seven grandchildren; and six great-grandchildren. He and Mary were buried in Marco Island Cemetery.

In 2022, Regan and Jennifer Weiss purchased the Sarazens' former residence at 7151 Jasmin Drive, designed by Thomas Reed Martin, for $780,000. Weiss is a founder and fractional chief marketing officer providing strategic marketing advice and leadership for projects for Hub Life Charities Inc. Regan installed a putting green in the rear garden of the property and a life-size cutout of Sarazen swinging his mighty sand wedge club. The couple, respectful of the home's history, also renovated the baths befitting its 1920s motif.

For each residence that survives, there is sadly one lost. The residence of Warren E. Burns at 7328 Burns Point Circle, designed by Thomas Reed Martin and later owned by Ken and Abby Misemer, was demolished in 2002.

18

THE HACIENDA FROM THE 1930s TO 1960s

The Hacienda changed ownership several times over the decades, and its busy winter season catering to northern visitors usually ranged from November to April or December to May.

In 1930, with the hotel under its original ownership, Frank R. Steel managed the hotel, with Leo Haag, the Swiss chef formerly of the Fresh Meadow Country Club in Flushing, New York, directing the cuisine.

As the Great Depression raged, Warren E. Burns, the head of the Hotel Company, reduced rates for the hotel's rooms and meals. In the fall of 1931, Mrs. I.N. Vickers, the proprietor of the Kentucky Inn on Grand Boulevard, took over the management of the hotel and dining room while Mrs. Oneta DeWoody hosted social activities. Chef Haag was expected to return, but no documentation of his return exists.

In 1935, the Hotel Company sold The Hacienda to Gray Holmes and Robert Holmes Jr., brothers with twenty years' experience as hoteliers who employed a staff of twenty-five. The brothers also operated a summer hotel in Helena, Georgia, and many satisfied winter guests of The Hacienda often spent their summers in the brothers' hotel in Georgia, as the same seasonal staff serviced both hotels.

During the Great Depression, the hotel dining room's seating capacity of one hundred served both hotel guests and locals, and the restaurant earned the reputation as the best eating establishment on Florida's west coast. Locals patronized the restaurant's weekly Saturday evening smorgasbords, featuring entertainment such as dances with a live orchestra and bingo

A postcard features the Hacienda Hotel, circa the late 1930s. *West Pasco Historical Society*.

Hotel guests gather on the north veranda, circa the 1940s. *West Pasco Historical Society*.

games, fashion shows and events associated with the city's annual spring Chasco Fiesta, culminating in the coronation ball, at which a local woman and man were crowned Queen Chasco and King Pithla.

The Holmes brothers engaged Major H.M. Stanford to operate The Hacienda. Stanford had previously operated the Hotel Tybee in Savannah Beach, the Tampa Bay Hotel (now the University of Tampa) and the DeSoto Hotel in downtown Tampa. In 1934, Stanford extended the hotel's winter season to May to increase revenue. That same year, the Holmes brothers introduced weekly Friday night dinner/bridge parties attended by the city's elite.

When the 1935 season ended, the Holmes brothers extended Stanford's lease for three years. During the off season, Stanford and his staff traveled north to a summer hotel in Connecticut. During Stanford's seasonal absence, Robert Simms operated The Hacienda for the summer months and prepared for major renovations that were scheduled for the following season.

The Hacienda enjoyed a prosperous season in 1939–40. Chef Armand Dybing's weekly Saturday evening Swedish smorgasbords increased in popularity, and the hotel then offered a gift shop in its lobby. By 1942, A.L. Palmer operated the hotel under the Holmes brothers' leadership.

During most of World War II, The Hacienda did not operate at capacity.

In November 1944, the Holmes brothers sold the hotel to Reverend Dr. William T. Watson, the pastor of a Christian and Missionary Alliance church in St. Petersburg who also founded the evangelical Trinity Bible School in Temple Terrace in 1932 (now Trinity College of Florida in Trinity). Dancing to the sound of Prohibition-era jazz and war-era swing in The Hacienda's lobby was now replaced by Dr. Watson's weekly religious services on Sundays.

While the hotel was under Watson's ownership, kitchen manager R.W. Ross created a memorable Christmas Day in 1944 that was open to the public. For $1.25, diners enjoyed a Florida cocktail or consommé, a relish tray, roast turkey with giblet gravy, cranberry sauce, glazed sweet potatoes or whipped potatoes, peas, carrots, squash, minced pie or sherbet, assorted breads and beverages.

In 1945, the Writers and Artists Workshop was held at The Hacienda under the direction of Winnifred Offord Long, the state president of the National League of Pen Women and a resident of St. Petersburg known as "the grand dame of Suncoast art." During the convention, Jessie E. Williams of Seattle, the writer of over fifty published poems, penned a sonnet about the hotel.

New Port Richey is especially well located for visitors coming into Florida by automobile . . . . being on U. S. Highway No. 19 (Fla. 210) which is the through short route south from Brooksville. Excellent highways open up exciting sight-seeing to you in all directions. Famous Moon Lake Gardens and Dude Ranch are only 9 miles from the Hacienda Hotel. New Port Richey is largely a resort community and you will see here many beautiful winter homes of prominent persons.

We invite you to come and enjoy with us this fine atmosphere of friendly hospitality and comfort; and whether you stay one day, a week or the entire season the same pleasing service is at your disposal.

AMERICAN PLAN
Rates begin at $5 daily, single.
$9 daily, double.

Weekly and seasonal rates on application.

GRAY HOLMES - ROBERT HOLMES, Jr.
Owners-Managers

A Hotel Whose Friendly Hospitality Will Please You

View of the Lobby Through to the Dining Rooms

Views of the Cotee River from Hotel Grounds

The Patio and Part of the Shady Hotel Lawn

THIS is an invitation to you to come and visit the Hacienda Hotel at New Port Richey, Florida, ... a friendly hotel, open November 15th to April 15th, which offers every conceivable modern comfort and convenience in an atmosphere of such charm and beauty that, once experienced, you will want to come again and again.

The Hacienda Hotel is one of the most beautiful smaller resort hotels in the Sunshine State . . . . . authentically Spanish in architecture and richness of appointments . . . . located on the banks of the tropical Cotee River . . . . with fifty guest rooms, each with private bath, solid carpeted floors, steam heat, telephones and available with either twin or double beds. Guest rooms are available singly or in combination en suite with sun parlors.

From your first glimpse of the Hacienda Hotel you will find an ever-increasing array of features appealing to your sense of beauty, your love for comfort, enjoyable environment and hospitality. You will delight in the true tropical splendor of the spacious grounds comprising acres of grassy lawns studded with shrubbery, palms and flowers. You will love the wide terraces, the arched doorways, the inviting balconies and the large patio.

You will find a new sense of luxury, relaxation and comfort in the big lobby with its massive open fireplace, with its large doorways opening on the terrace on one side and the cloister on the other. Hacienda Hotel service is planned to anticipate, inobtrusively, your every need for comfort and entertainment whether you come to rest or to enjoy outdoor sports and recreations.

The dining room of the Hacienda Hotel enjoys a splendid reputation along the west coast of Florida. A cuisine of variety, freshness and goodness tempts your appetite for every meal.

Outdoor sports have always attracted Hacienda guests. The Cotee River bordering the grounds offers some of Florida's finest fresh and salt water fishing. It is only two miles from the hotel dock to the open Gulf of Mexico and the hotel maintains a 28-foot launch as well as small boats for the use of guests. Within the hotel grounds are shuffleboard courts, putting greens and tennis courts. Only a few miles away is the Tarpon Springs golf course and within 30 to 45 minutes drive from the hotel are Tampa, Clearwater and St. Petersburg with all their numerous attractions.

Opposite, top: The Hacienda Hotel's brochure during its management by the Holmes brothers boasts an American meal plan and accommodation rates starting at five dollars a day. *West Pasco Historical Society.*

Opposite, bottom: The Hacienda Hotel's brochure during its management by the Holmes brothers specifies its season ran from November 15 to April 15. *West Pasco Historical Society.*

This page, top: The hotel's east entrance, circa the 1940s. *West Pasco Historical Society.*

This page, bottom: The Hacienda Hotel, January 1948. *West Pasco Historical Society.*

The Hacienda Hotel, circa the 1940s. *West Pasco Historical Society.*

During the postwar era of the late 1940s and 1950s, The Hacienda remained the city's premier hostelry and social and cultural center. It featured prominently in the lives of local citizens who attended dances, musical concerts and weddings there. Many danced beneath its glittering black iron chandeliers in the same way motion picture stars had done so in the late 1920s and early 1930s.

The Hacienda served as a venue for local clubs and organizations' events, such as the Women's Club annual tea and garden party, the Rhode Island

Top: Gulf High School students engage in a group dance at the 1952 prom in the Hacienda Hotel's lobby. *West Pasco Historical Society*.

Bottom: An event in the Hacienda's dining room, circa 1950. *West Pasco Historical Society*.

A ladies' organization meets in the hotel's dining room, circa 1948. *West Pasco Historical Society*.

Guests socialize in the hotel's lobby at the wedding reception of Walt and Lauzanne Casson, 1955. *West Pasco Historical Society*.

Club of New Port Richey's annual supper and meeting for the town's former residents and those visiting from the northern states, the Chasco Junior Women's Club's annual Mother's Day tea, the Women's Association of Community Church's annual Washington's Birthday Silver Tea, the New Port Richey Volunteer Fire Department's annual firemen's ball and Gulf High School's annual homecoming dance and football team banquets and its proms and graduation dinner/dance.

The Junior Chamber of Commerce and the Better Business Club met at The Hacienda, and its advertisements for the Baptist Bible Conferences declared, "You don't have to be a Baptist," and invited non-Baptists to attend and bring their Bibles.

The Hacienda Hotel, circa the 1940s. *West Pasco Historical Society*.

Aside from hosting conferences and conventions, the hotel served as a venue for weddings, first holy communions and special family celebrations.

The hotel's tradition of Saturday night smorgasbords maintained popularity in the 1940s. The dinner, priced at one dollar, often included Bingo games.

Reverend Watson Holds Religious Services in the Hotel's Lobby

Reverend Watson, who continued to conduct vespers in the hotel's lobby each Sunday, campaigned for the city to purchase the structure and repurpose it as a college. In 1961, Watson's Trinity College inhabited the former Fenway Hotel in Dunedin (returned to a hotel in 2018) before it was moved to its campus in Trinity.

In May 1950, Watson sold The Hacienda to H.W. and Evelyn Schuldt of Omaha, Nebraska. The new owners' renovations included the addition of a coffee shop.

Following this transaction, the Hacienda Hotel changed ownership several times in the 1950s.

A Legal Battle Between Two Lovers Over The Hacienda

By 1953, The Hacienda was owned by two couples, Philip and Rebecca Merkatz and Morris and Anna Gates. The Merkatzes had previously owned the Royall Inn in Woodbourne, New York, and the Gateses had owned Delaware Towers in Chicago.

A January 1954 advertisement for "The New Hacienda Hotel" promoted charcoal-grilled steaks, the ultimate in cuisine, and entertainment in the cocktail lounge. The owners also announced plans for the construction of a seventy-five-foot-long swimming pool on property across Main Street with a canopy walkway, but this never materialized. A legal suit between the two couples soon appeared in the newspapers, and subsequently, the hotel changed hands again.

The next sale of the hotel led to a bizarre story involving a star sapphire ring, a $6,000 mink coat and two former lovers who took center stage in a financial dispute over the hotel at the Tampa Federal Courthouse. Ironically, the 1905 courthouse on Florida Avenue was repurposed to become Le Méridien Boutique Hotel in 2013. In fact, a courtroom witness stand now serves as the maître d' stand in the hotel's dining room.

A postcard dated 1956 features the Hacienda Hotel's south courtyard. *West Pasco Historical Society*.

In April 1955, the legal battle between The Hacienda's owner Maxine Stein and her former lover Raymond Miller made headlines in the *Tampa Tribune*. Miller filed in federal court a suit for the appointment of a receiver for the hotel, the hotel's sale and the dissolution of the partnership that owned it. Miller charged Maxine Stein, described as a trim, husky-voiced widow from Chicago, for defrauding him of his investment in the hotel.

Miller claimed he purchased a half interest in the hotel from Mr. and Mrs. Gates in June 1953 for $15,000 in cash and a balance in notes. Subsequently, the Gateses purchased the other half interest from Mr. and Mrs. Merkatz. In December 1953, the Gateses sold their half interest to Stein. Miller's suit claimed he agreed to sell his half interest to Stein for $20,000 in February 1955, but she paid him only $5,000 and stated she would not pay any more.

Miller accused Stein of defrauding him of the $15,000 due on the purchase price and $5,500 that he had spent on renovations. Stein claimed she and Miller had planned to marry and that she had gifted him a $2,500 sapphire ring. She also claimed Miller had purchased the hotel for her because he loved her.

Finally, a federal judge granted Stein complete ownership of The Hacienda after she paid Miller $5,000.

The Mid-Century Semple Era

Maxine Stein sold The Hacienda to Francis Supic of Milwaukee for $100,000 in September 1955. Supic reopened the hotel with her son, Karl Gabriel, as manager.

On Christmas Day 1955, Lauzanne Sims and Walt Casson held their wedding reception at The Hacienda, and the bride threw her wedding bouquet from the stairway in the lobby to an attractive group of single women.

On March 27, 1959, newspapers announced that Supic had sold The Hacienda to Richard Semple, the former manager of the Pinellas Poultry Company who was originally from Ohio. Semple; his wife, Jeane Marie; and their children, Barbara Jean, Robert Jr. and William, lived in Tarpon Springs. Semple closed the hotel in July for six weeks of extensive remodeling on the first floor. The Semples redecorated and refurbished the hotel in 1959 and did so again in 1961.

Lauzanne Sims Casson tosses her bridal bouquet in the Hacienda Hotel's lobby during her wedding reception, December 25, 1955. *West Pasco Historical Society.*

Female guests of all ages attend to the wedding cake and refreshment table during the reception of Walt and Lauzanne Casson at the Hacienda Hotel, December 25, 1955. *West Pasco Historical Society.*

Robert and Jean Marie Semple purchased the Hacienda Hotel in 1959. *Photograph by Angelo Deciucies, West Pasco Historical Society.*

Richard Semple renamed and rebranded the dining hall as the La Fonda Steak Room and renamed the cocktail lounge behind it the Matador Room, with bullfight posters displayed on the walls. Servers wore toreador pants and bolero jackets. Chef Henry Weber, formerly of the Fort Harrison Hotel in Clearwater, enhanced the food policy of the dining room. The Semples hosted a ribbon-cutting ceremony and dinner/dance on October 3, 1959, which was extensively photographed by Angelo Deciucies.

In May 1960, Semple announced plans to construct a large swimming pool with funds raised by the sale of memberships. Use of the pool would be restricted to members and hotel guests. These plans were never realized.

In 1961, Semple expanded the hotel's services for the increasing number of retirees settling in Pasco County. He advertised The Hacienda as an economical and luxurious "retirement hotel" for $125 a month for a "basic single with a bath." Semple boasted "one of the finest dining rooms on the west coast" and offered to "paint your room your favorite color."

The Hacienda remained a headquarters for downtown businesspeople for lunch, coffee breaks and cocktail happy hours. For decades, buffet-style meals were served in the hotel's dining room. Locals returned to the hotel for senior class proms, sports banquets, weddings and community club meetings. This trend continued for generations.

Opposite, top: City officials attend Robert Semple's ribbon cutting event at the opening of the Matador Room at the hotel, October 3, 1959. *Photograph by Angelo Deciucies, West Pasco Historical Society.*

Opposite, bottom: During special events, dining spilled into the hotel's lobby. *Photograph by Angelo Deciucies, West Pasco Historical Society.*

Right: Robert Semple's Matador Room features a Spanish toreador theme exemplified by this vintage hotel coaster. *West Pasco Historical Society.*

Below: The hotel bar originally occupied the current private north dining room. *Photograph by Angelo Deciucies, West Pasco Historical Society.*

Left, top: The lobby features a telephone booth in its southeast corner. *Photograph by Angelo Deciucies, West Pasco Historical Society.*

Left, bottom: The original stairway to the second floor extends into the lobby and features twisted Mediterranean columns, Thomas Reed Martin's signature architectural motif. *Photograph by Angelo Deciucies, West Pasco Historical Society.*

Opposite, top: Chef Henry Weber carves and serves a roasted pig, 1959. *Photograph by Angelo Deciucies, West Pasco Historical Society.*

Opposite, bottom: The dramatic arch to the Hacienda Hotel's dining room is visible from the lobby, where an overflow of guests dine, 1959. *Photo by Angelo Deciucies, West Pasco Historical Society.*

Above: Hotel dinner guests attend the opening of the Matador Room, 1959. *Photograph by Angelo Deciucies, West Pasco Historical Society*.

Left: City mayor Clair Kohler, city officials and male citizens gather in The Hacienda's courtyard, 1950s. *Photograph by Angelo Diciucies, West Pasco Historical Society.*

The Hacienda Hotel hosts a dance reception in the hotel's lobby during the city's annual Chasco Fiesta, circa 1960. *Photograph by Angelo Deciucies, West Pasco Historical Society.*

The crowning of a king and queen is held at the Hacienda Hotel during the Chasco Fiesta of 1962. *Right to left*: Beva Stevenson, Nancy Lavo, Janet Briggs, B.J. Semple, Theresa Stover, Polly Snell, Joan Cummings, Steve Uzzle, Cary Crutchfield, Terry Little, Bill Colbert, Tom Dixon, Tim Slater and Mike Park. *West Pasco Historical Society.*

The Legend of The Hacienda Being Won in a Poker Game

Dr. Chase DeCubellis, a board-certified doctor of chiropractic medicine and the owner of Beyond Bones Chiropractic and Wellness, shared with this author a legend about his great-uncle William Desmond "Des" Little (1913–1989) winning The Hacienda in a poker game.

Little owned Desmond Little and Sons Paving and contributed to the building of West Pasco Hospital and the Gulf High School football stadium, which was named for him. Des and his wife, Michaeline "Mickey" DeCubellis (1914–2009), resided on Little Road, which was also named for him. The Littles cultivated close personal relationships with Johnny Cash and June Carter and Reverend Billy Graham, all of whom visited the Hacienda Hotel in the 1970s.

When Des and Michaeline's oldest son, Desmond Gene, married Linda Jeanne Grey, the daughter of James E. Grey, in August 1962, the couple's wedding ceremony was held at The Hacienda.

According to newspaper articles, in the late 1960s, Richard Semple sold a portion of his ownership of The Hacienda to Des Little and two other partners. According to the recollection of Jackie Battista, she and her former

A postcard dated January 24, 1968, depicts the Hacienda Hotel in its third decade. *West Pasco Historical Society.*

husband later purchased the business from a partnership of four individuals, including Semple and Little.

The hotel's first floor was expanded in the rear for additional dining; the arched veranda was enclosed and an additional structure with picture windows overlooking Sims Park was built.

On June 6, 1968, a fire occurred at The Hacienda in the early morning hours. All twenty-seven residents quickly evacuated without injury. Twelve guest rooms sustained major damage, with a 10 percent loss of the forty-seven-year-old building. Fire sprinkler systems were not required by code at the time.

The Semples retained ownership of The Hacienda until the city's approaching half-century celebration in 1974, at which time, ownership of the hotel was passed to Mike and Jackie Battista, ushering in a new era.

19

THE BATTISTA ERA

When The Hacienda was reopened as a boutique hotel in September 2022, decades after its closure, this author met with members of the Battista family, who had returned to their former combination home and business to see its restoration. They reminisced about both raising children and growing up within the context of operating a family business, staging entertainment and hosting entertainers. The interview is available on YouTube.

In 1974, Mike and Jackie Battista relocated from windy Chicago to tropical New Port Richey with their five children, Michael Jr., Nick, John, Tina and Michele. As a Max Factor executive who traveled across the country, Mike Sr. had set his eyes on the former Pink Lady on Main Street—then painted pearl white—during his family vacations in New Port Richey to visit Jackie's parents, John and Irene Scalzetti. When the hotel was listed for sale, Jackie's father immediately informed the couple.

Shortly before the city's semicentennial, Mike and Jackie purchased The Hacienda—well past its prime—from Robert Semple, Desmond Little and two other partners. While Mike worked in California, Jackie drove from Chicago to Florida with her cousin Sharon and their combined eight children in an old Lincoln towing a small van. Sharon had agreed to assist Jackie in operating the hotel's restaurant and lounge.

Mike and Jackie removed the bullfighting motif and constructed an ornamental wall that enclosed the hotel's open courtyard and created a barrier from its front parking lot. In the 1970s, their nightly guest room rate

The Hacienda Hotel's former owner, Jackie Battista Jackson, returns to the hotel with her family in September 2002. *Left to right*: John Battista, Michele Battista Hulmes, Jackie Battista Jackson and Tina Battista Bartunek, September 2022. *Author's collection*.

was $27, and the hotel restaurant served a one-and-a-half-pound lobster dinner for $8.95, which included unlimited trips to the salad bar.

Initially, the Battista family lived in the part of the hotel that is currently called "the bordello rooms," located over the kitchen. However, in conservative New Port Richey in the twentieth century, no part of The Hacienda ever operated as a bordello. This part of the structure contained the former quarters of the maids and chauffeurs of the early guests, not sex workers.

The red wallpaper and paneling discovered in the so-called bordello rooms during the restoration were assumed evidence of sexual activities during the Prohibition era. However, John Battista remembers driving with his father to Chicago to bring the wallpaper and paneling back to New Port Richey for installation in the 1970s.

Originally, there was no fountain in the courtyard. Mike's sons, John and Nick, installed it. "When a Spanish-style building was demolished in Ybor City," John recalled, "my father sent us to get the brick and bring it back here. Nick and I relocated and set each brick in place to construct a path around the fountain."

The hotel hosted many wedding ceremonies of local couples in the courtyard between the fountain and a gazebo. During Gulf Junior High School proms, the hotel's dining tables overflowed to the verandas behind the arches surrounding the courtyard.

The original front desk was located where the elevator now exists and contained a vault. The original entrance on Bank Street, which exists today, had been closed prior to the Battista area. This space, now occupied by the entrance and some restrooms, had been converted into three additional guest rooms. Phone booths were located in the lobby by the stairs, across from the front desk, and in the lounge. During their interview with this author, all the family members immediately recalled and recited the hotel's phone number: 849-6161.

After completing refurbishment, with inspiration from their Italian heritage, Mike and Jackie focused on elevating the cuisine of the hotel's restaurant and returning the hotel to its roots as a cultural and social center with fine cuisine and entertainment. They brought on board chef Gerry Leslie from Alaska, self-described as an "Okie from Muskogee" who had been chief chef at the Ketchikan Elks Club.

On October 24, 1974, the fiftieth anniversary of the incorporation of New Port Richey was celebrated with a dinner at the Hacienda Hotel. The menu—turkey, cornbread, corn and all the trimmings—duplicated the dinner served at the opening of the hotel in 1927.

FAMOUS ENTERTAINERS PERFORMING AT THE HACIENDA

When this author asked the Battista family to identify their happiest memories of the hotel, there was consensus. Tina Battista Bartunek replied, "The parties." Jackie Battista Jackson responded, "The Chasco Fiesta events."

"The performances by the Ink Spots," John added as one of his favorite memories, "and Tiny Tim. We had Frankie Fontaine, Guy Lombardo, Rudy Vallée with his megaphone—Rudy Vallée was somewhat challenging."

"Frankie Fontaine was not on his best behavior," Jackie said politely.

"Tiny Tim was the best," John recalled with fondness.

"He was the gentleman," remembered Jackie.

All members of the family described Tiny as the warmest, most approachable and likable of headliners ever booked at their venue. He put on a stunning show and sang with gusto.

"Tiny Tim only played the ukulele and sang in a falsetto voice when he performed 'Tiptoe through the Tulips,' the 1920s song," John explained. "The rest of the show, he was down on his knee, sweating and singing."

"He had a beautiful voice," Jackie interjected.

"He was the greatest entertainer," John asserted, "and the crowd went wild."

"Here's a funny story about what John did at twelve years old," Jackie giggled. "He put on a wig and got a little ukulele and did the Tiny Tim imitation in the restaurant. And here comes Tiny himself. He absolutely loved it!"

Tiny Tim was beloved by this family five decades later.

"Tiny Tim did several shows for us," John said. "He was the best. He was so cool. He also had a healthy appetite. He wanted a pound of spaghetti, a tray of eggplant parmesan and loaves of bread. We'd take it up to his room."

The family's affection for the eccentric entertainer was echoed by a local newspaper headline: "His Hair Is 'Kinky,' His Suits Don't Fit, and His Fans Love Him."

Tiny Tim (1932–1996), whose real name was Herbert Butros Khaury, made several appearances on Dan Rowan and Dick Martin's television variety show *Laugh-In* in the late 1960s. In 1969, he married seventeen-year-old Victoria Budinger, known as Miss Vicki, on *The Tonight Show*, starring Johnny Carson, with forty million people watching. The couple divorced four years later.

"We were told by Tiny Tim's publicist not to say anything about Miss Vicki," Jackie said. "Then Thad Lowry, who owned WGUL radio station, came in, and the first thing he said to Tiny Tim was, 'What's the thing with Miss Vicki?'"

"I would bring his laundry to the laundromat," Jackie recalled, "and the workers would be so excited to be doing Tiny Tim's laundry."

"We have a family photo with all us kids and Tiny Tim," Michele Battista Hulmes announced.

Frankie Fontaine (1920–1978), who did not impress the family as much as Tiny had, appeared on early television programs like *The Jack Benny Show*, *The Jackie Gleason Show* and *The Ed Sullivan Show*. The comedian and baritone singer usually portrayed an inebriated, comedic character, Crazy Guggenheim. His trademark was a bug-eyed grin and silly laugh.

"We'd open the lobby and dining room for big events," John explained. "We sold so many tickets that we'd set up rows of seating. We created the stage by the proscenium arch near the front desk or in front of the fireplace. Rudy Vallée and Frankie Fontaine performed in front of the fireplace."

"The Ink Spots were the best," Jackie asserted. "Great guys."

"When our band would rehearse," John remembered, "they'd coach us. We were singing 'Proud Mary,' and they said, 'Stop right there.' They joined in with harmony. We still perform it that way today, thanks to the Ink Spots."

The Ink Spots vocal pop group dominated radio and record sales in the 1930s and 1940s. Their musical style predated the rhythm and blues, rock and roll and doo-wop genres. The group appealed to white and Black communities during this era, known for its racism and segregation. After the Ink Spots disbanded in 1954, many second- and third-generation vocal groups that called themselves "The Ink Spots" emerged, both with and without members of the original group.

Michele suddenly interjected, "Remember the New Year's Eve party when Dad had all the psychics?" With a fifty-plus-year history, the hotel had plenty of ghost stories and active supernatural phenomena to give the clairvoyants material.

During the Battista era at the hotel, the most memorable New Year's Eve event took place over a weekend in February 1977, not December 31, when Guy Lombardo (1902–1977) and his Royal Canadian Orchestra performed four times in two days. Bandleader Lombardo earned the moniker "Mr. New Year's Eve," and his orchestra became synonymous with the holiday.

The Royal Canadian Orchestra, at the Roosevelt Hotel in New York City in 1929, played radio's first nationwide New Year's Eve broadcast, which popularized "Auld Lang Syne." The orchestra played in that location until 1959, and from then until 1976 it played at the Waldorf Astoria Hotel. Live television broadcasts of their performances were a large part of New Year's celebrations across North America, as millions watched the show with their friends at house parties. An overflowing crowd of New Port Richey's retirees flocked to see this iconic act. Newspapers reported The Hacienda's ballroom was "bulging at the seams" as dancers spilled onto the veranda.

Other than the memories of the lavish entertainment and performances, the Battista family agreed, everything else was hard work.

"We were maids, books, bartenders," John clarified.

The Permanent Guests

When the Battista family toured a double queen guest room, no. 116, and marveled about its appointments, Michelle murmured, "I cleaned this room more than a few times."

As she walked through the newly restored, grand lobby, Michele said, "I can see Grandma Irene and Aunt Emma washing all these windows."

Jackie's father, John Scalzetti, also assisted in operating the hotel.

The first-floor wing was reserved for year-round house guests who had transitioned from the previous owner. These permanent guests, mostly elderly, could not climb their stairs, and there was no elevator.

Gertrude Dean, who first visited The Hacienda in 1943, lived there during the Battista reign. She and her husband resided at the hotel until they purchased a home. After her husband's death, Gertrude returned as a permanent resident.

"Their rent covered breakfast, lunch and dinner and cleaning services," John explained. "The guest rooms had transoms that opened over the doors, and the baths had the original clawfoot tubs."

In 1975, the hotel's restaurant served a roast prime rib dinner for $7.50 and Jackie's homemade ravioli for $2.95. Sometimes, the prime rib was served with ravioli.

In May 1977, Mike Battista obtained a license from the State Department of Health and Rehabilitative Services to permit The Hacienda to operate as an adult congregate living facility, allowing individuals to live at the hotel with government subsidy assistance. The Pasco Housing Authority determined twenty of the hotel's rooms were eligible for subsidized rent.

"We now offer somebody making under $200 a month a chance to live like a king," Battista told the *Tampa Bay Times*. Competing with modern hotels on U.S. 19, the Battistas began renting on a long-term basis to the elderly, but the new license allowed these residents to live at a more affordable rate.

The hotel had catered to older residents since about 1961, but the license ensured more stringent sanitation and safety standards, including regular state inspections. A resident's eligibility required they be ambulatory, and their supportive services included transportation services. Even pets were allowed. "We're here to treat people like we'll expect to be treated once we reach a certain age," Mike declared.

For $250 a month, residents of the hotel received personal service and three meals a day in the dining room. Government subsidies reduced that price to $160 a month. A two-room suite was priced at $550.

The Hacienda's Golden Anniversary Celebration

In 1977, the Battistas celebrated the hotel's fiftieth anniversary, and the event was attended by James E. Grey, a longtime resident and realtor, and Julie Obenreder. Obenreder supplied Jackie Battista with vintage 1920s finery for the period costume affair.

Obenreder, a nurse who relocated to New Port Richey in 1945 with her husband and children, befriended the Battista family and shared stories of the city's past. She donated her services to deliver at least fifty babies for the Black residents of Pine Hill, where, previously, the only option was home delivery. Obenreder also promoted the community's history by researching and writing *West Pasco Heritage* and *My Pioneer Days in West Pasco*. In 1973, she helped found the West Pasco Historical Society and assisted in acquiring the society's headquarters, a former schoolhouse.

The Hotel as a Music Venue

If you are an adolescent boy involved in a garage band, there's no better venue to rehearse and perform than your parents' historic hotel lobby with a high ceiling that allows for rich acoustics. In the early 1980s, John Battista's band Shadowfax, formed with Gulf High School classmates Tony Clark, Barry Horvath, Mike Napoli, Russ Tanner, Frank Timpanelli and Mike Vaporis, played in the hotel's lobby. Just as the grand lobby was transformed into a dance floor in the 1920s through the 1960s, it served as a disco floor with a DJ booth in the 1980s.

In July 1977, Mike and Jackie invited local talents Jimmy Ferraro, Ginger Ramsey and Lee and Cheryl Bredenbeck to perform at the hotel. Ferraro, a twenty-year-old theater aficionado, directed and performed *Night on Broadway*, a revue of iconic musical numbers from the Great White Way in the grand ballroom lobby of the hotel. With a cost of $5.95 for a buffet dinner and a show, the event was sold out. Its success spurred another revue directed by Ferraro, *Let Us Entertain You*, for which the price was increased by $1.

In 1982, The Hacienda made headlines in the *Tampa Tribune* when Mike and Jackie introduced their own dinner theater concept to the hotel. The dinner special included prime rib, a baked potato, vegetables and a salad bar priced at $12.95. The first production was the long-running off-Broadway show *The Fantasticks*.

Bizarre Occurrences and Ghost Stories

Operating a hotel provides many opportunities for strange and bizarre incidents, experiences and occurrences.

None quite compared with the day Mike Battista gathered his sons to clean the remnants of what he described as a wild pizza party in the room next to the former tower guestroom. The guests who checked out had trashed the guest room by throwing pizza on the walls and carpeting. Battista instructed his sons to don rubber gloves and bring buckets of bleach water and scrub brushes for a deep clean. Although the room has been reconfigured and renumbered, the "pizza room" is likely the current guest room no. 326.

As the brothers removed what they were told was mozzarella cheese, pepperoni and tomato sauce, they realized the consistency of the material did not resemble food. It looked more like brain matter and skull fragments. A guest had ended his life with a firearm, and the authorities overlooked sending in a biohazard cleaning crew. John Battista acknowledges his father could sometimes be a character.

"The basement was creepy," Michele said. "But despite what others reported after the hotel was closed, there were no caged rooms in our basement!" Nor were there tunnels to the nearby river for the smuggling of bootleg liquor.

Over the years, the family experienced the hotel's lights turning on and off without human intervention and pounding on the walls and windows overlooking Sims Park, usually at night. Initially, these occurrences caused Mike Battista to return to the hotel with his firearm, suspecting an intruder. After multiple episodes, the family accepted their occupancy likely overlapped with unexplained spiritual energy and learned to live harmoniously with their unregistered "guests."

Michele remembered following a hotel housekeeper into a guest room to begin cleaning when she was about five or six. The housekeeper gasped and pushed the child out of the room. However, Michele caught a traumatic glimpse of a man in a dark suit and shiny black dress shoes hanging in the closet. In the early 1990s, Russ Tanner, a band member of Shadowfax and one of John Battista's closest friends, unknowingly spent the night after a performance in the guest room in which this man tragically took his own life. Tanner recalled waking in that night and observing a vision of disembodied, shiny black shoes levitating off the floor. He ran downstairs to report the event. Later, the family explained the sad event that had occurred in the space a few years prior and concluded the elevated shoes may have been at the height the man's shoes were when he was found hanging from a closet rod.

When the family invited a group of clairvoyants to investigate the hotel, the psychic experts immediately responded as they approached this room from the corridor. "They went bananas upon reaching this space," John recalled. The "hanging shadow" room is currently guest room no. 338, the most paranormally active room during the hotel's recent restoration, according to the construction crew and staff.

Not all The Hacienda's disturbances are spiritual in nature.

"We were in the bar one night and heard a big thump," Jackie said. "Some fellow jumped out of a third-floor window."

"He landed and rolled, uninjured," John explained. "Then stood up and walked away, headed to the bar."

THE COMMUNITY'S WATERING HOLE

The Hacienda's lounge was located at the north end of the dining room, which now serves as a private dining space overlooking Sims Park. As this author joined members of the Battista family for lunch, they reminisced about the space in the 1970s and 1980s.

"The bar was small and crowded," Jackie said. "It was so popular, you couldn't get in. It was three people deep every single night and had a jukebox. Then we moved the bar to another location. Our staff knew every customer's favorite drink. As customers drove into the parking lot, the staff would say, 'There's the Crown Royale. There's the scotch and water.'"

"Everyone in town came to this bar," John remarked. "The Bazulli brothers [who built two three-story buildings on the northwest and southeast corners of Grand Boulevard and Gulf Drive], Billy Pasco [a descendant of Samuel Pasco] and Dr. Wilfred Neil [the town historian]."

"George 'Bud' Brown, president of Pasco Water Authority," Jackie continued, "and Orville Williamson of the Pasco County Sheriff's Department. All the judges used to come for lunch."

"Richard Milbauer was here every single weekday," John said.

"Richard had breakfast here every day," Jackie interjected. "He introduced my son John to Johnny Cash to cut a record."

Richard Milbauer (1933–1981) was a Gulf High School graduate and prominent attorney in practice in New Port Richey. He was a member of the American Bar Association, Florida Bar Association and West Pasco Bar Association. Milbauer was involved in local politics and was a five-term member of New Port Richey City Council during the 1960s and 1970s. The attorney's father, Michael Milbauer (1894–1964), was a real estate agent, insurance agent, philanthropist and one of the founders of First Federal Savings and Loan of Pasco County. He operated an office on Main Street that had previously been occupied by Reginald Sims.

"Robert K. Hicks, our humanities teacher from Gulf High, was here every day," John laughed. "If people needed to see Mr. Hicks, they'd come here to The Hacienda bar."

"This was the city's meeting place, that's for sure," Jackie proudly remembered.

Regularly, patrons would see the city's mayor, chief of police and sheriff at The Hacienda's bar. Once, when an intoxicated customer became disruptive, Jackie had to sternly order him to leave. She was surprised that the customer complied without protest. Then Jackie turned around to see, standing behind her, all three city authorities backing up her authority.

Johnny Cash and Reverend Billy Graham

"We loved the Little family and the DeCubellis family," John Battista said with affection. "Des Little and his son Pete were here every day."

"Johnny Cash lived down the river on Sunset Boulevard," Michele Battista Hulmes told this author. "I played with the Cash kids when they came to visit." Cash (1932–2003), a legendary country musician-singer-songwriter, and his wife, June Carter, had inherited a modest home in New Port Richey upon the death of June's mother, Maybelle Carter.

Des Little, Jackie and Mike's friend, was also friends with Johnny Cash. Little and Cash took fishing trips together in the Gulf of Mexico.

"One Friday night, Des comes over," Jackie recalled about her first meeting with the musical icon. "Des says, 'Jackie, come over, I'm going to introduce you to some people.' We were really busy, and my ex-husband probably said, 'You can leave now. You need to make the apple sauce.' So, Des finally drags me off to the river beside the hotel. Guess who we were going to meet—whose boat just pulled out—Johnny Cash, Reverend Billy Graham and his wife, Ruth Graham. And I'm waving goodbye to them!"

Reverend Billy Graham (1918–2018) was an evangelist and an ordained Southern Baptist minister who became well known internationally in the late 1940s and became involved in politics and with politicians.

Johnny Cash enjoyed a cocktail at The Hacienda when he and June performed for a Police Benevolent benefit at Gulf Comprehensive High School's gymnasium in November 1980.

The Last Days of the First Incarnation of The Hacienda

By the 1980s, Mike and Jackie Battista had divorced. In 1986, the Hacienda Hotel passed from the Battista family to Gulf Coast Jewish Family Services.

Mike Battista, who honorably served as a U.S. Marine, was a serial entrepreneur who passionately engaged in a wide range of businesses as an owner, consultant and visionary. After refurbishing and operating the Hacienda Hotel, he helped lead the resurgence of Ybor City in the 1990s

Members of the extended Battista family visit The Hacienda in September 2022. *Author's collection.*

as the owner and operator of Rough Riders Restaurant. Battista died in 2021. Battista's family honored his memory with an engraved brick set in a pathway that leads from The Hacienda's dining terrace to Sims Park.

While Mike often received credit for The Hacienda's success, Jackie balanced raising their children while she managed the hotel, restaurant and bar, working long hours in a demanding environment. When the hotel became successful, Mike left his position at Max Factor and operated the hotel full time.

Jackie developed a vast network of business and professional contacts through the hotel; after her divorce, she left The Hacienda and worked for Carl Minieri, a home builder and commercial developer of West Pasco County, and Pasco Water Authority. Jackie remarried and eventually retired to Vero Beach, Florida, where she currently enjoys being a grandmother.

The Hacienda's Battista era is affectionately remembered as its second golden age.

20

HACIENDA HOME FOR SPECIAL SERVICES

B y the 1980s, New Port Richey's aging population was living longer and required specialized care. Although many in this demographic needed medical supervision, they did not require expensive and restrictive twenty-four-hour nursing care. Gulf Coast Jewish Family Services (GCJFS) responded to this need by providing a less-restrictive level of care by transforming the former hotel into a licensed adult residential treatment facility.

Incentivized to reduce state costs, the Florida legislature appropriated $459,000 to convert the once-luxurious hotel into a care center. The reception desk area and vault (currently the location of the hotel's elevator) were converted into a medical records department, and a nursing station was constructed on the second-floor mezzanine, near the steps to the third floor.

In May 1986, The Hacienda reopened as the Hacienda Home for Special Services, a 110-bed residential center for individuals recovering from illness or surgery who were expected to return home within six months. Michael Bernstein, the executive director of Gulf Coast Jewish Family Services who founded the program, told the *Tampa Tribune* that The Hacienda could rescue seniors from getting trapped in costly nursing homes.

In media interviews, Bernstein described rehabilitative care as an "innovative and compassionate program" involving physical therapy, speech therapy and mental health counseling. Governor Bob Graham attended the opening gala and hailed the treatment concept.

The Hacienda's location promoted the residents' socialization and access to the downtown area, which offered opportunities to walk in Sims Park and window shop along Main Street and Grand Boulevard. By its launch, the

Hacienda Home's beds were already occupied, and the facility had a waiting list of about forty patients.

In 1987, in a move to prevent seniors with severe and persistent mental illness from languishing in state psychiatric hospitals and transition to more humane community placement, the Florida legislature established the Geriatric Residential Treatment System. By 1991, the Hacienda Home had expanded its services to deinstitutionalize this population. The program's goal was to transition patients from state hospitals to the former hotel and eventually to independent living with wraparound support services. The facility's treatment team included a psychiatrist, psychiatric nurses, psychotherapists and case managers. Day treatment services were delivered on site in an extension of the building behind the lobby. The program was a sweeping success. Fewer than 10 percent of the over seven hundred individuals placed at Hacienda Home returned to the state hospital.

Since the Hacienda Home was an open treatment facility, its residents were free to sign out and stroll in the community. Most of the residents were prescribed psychotropic medications to reduce their mental health symptoms of psychosis (delusions and hallucinations), anxiety, depression and mood fluctuations. During this era, many of these medications had side effects. The monthlong Chasco Fiesta, an annual downtown celebration of street parades, concerts, art fairs, loud music and large crowds became a safety issue for vulnerable residents.

Caroline Serra Henderson was employed by GCJFS and worked at the Hacienda Home. Hired in 1986 by Sheila Lopez, the chief financial officer, Caroline originally served as the director of medical records and designed and implemented its system. In 1989, she began working at the Hacienda Home, where her responsibilities were expanded, and she became the administrator of the organization's entire medical records department, a risk manager and a privacy officer.

"I, along with many dedicated Gulf Coast employees, worked together to help others," Caroline recalled with passion during an interview in the hotel's current restaurant, Sasha's on the Park, in December 2023. "The hotel's original vault housed the medical records department, and the nursing station was located behind the current front desk area. The hotel's tower area was where we stored and secured the residents' personal property. One of my offices with ornate windows overlooking Bank Street was on the top floor on the south side of the building."

"Behind the kitchen area," Caroline continued, "steps lead to a short floor of four offices with distinctive red paneling. These spaces served as officers for the case managers. The staff referred to them as the bordello rooms and wondered if that was their purpose when the building operated as a hotel."

Today, Caroline enjoys visiting the Hacienda Hotel and attending its special events. "I love coming back to this lovely building, which was a part of my career and life," she told this author. "I enjoy its beauty and history, and now, I'm a part of that history. It's remarkable that the hotel's unique features that we loved while working here—the fireplace, chandeliers and beamed ceiling—have been meticulously restored."

Ghost Stories

During its years as a care center for the aged and those with severe mental illness, the former hotel experienced numerous and frequent deaths. Many of the ghost stories associated with the hotel originated from this era. Sadly, in 1988, the body of an elderly female patient was found in Orange Lake shortly after she was observed eating breakfast at the Hacienda Home. The woman's walker was found by a tree at the edge of the lake.

"We operated as a 24/7 residential treatment facility," Caroline explained, "and at night, the building could feel creepy. The hallways were dimly illuminated. Night staff would often hear unexplained noises. That's where Mathilda was born. Mathilda definitely had a presence at The Hacienda."

"Everyone who worked here knew about Mathilda," Caroline asserted, "especially those on the night shift. While residents slept, we'd hear doors open and footsteps. But when we checked on the residents to find the source of the strange noises, they were asleep, and no one was roaming the hallways. We all knew without a doubt of the spiritual activity on the third-floor wing."

Sue Gleeson, Caroline's long-term employee and friend, frequently worked at night and recounted ghost stories about Mathilda. Long before working at the Hacienda Home, Sue was married at the Hacienda Hotel, where her wedding reception took place.

Michael Bernstein's Legacy

After working for over two decades at the Hacienda Home, Caroline resigned to pursue other interests in the acute care setting. Caroline said,

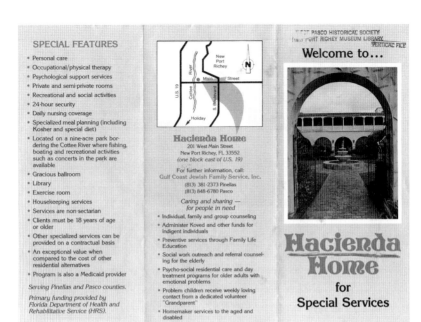

A brochure for the Hacienda Home outlines the special services provided in the former hotel in the 1980s. *West Pasco Historical Society.*

The Hacienda Home operated in the former hotel from the 1980s until the early 2000s. *West Pasco Historical Society.*

For many years, I reported directly to Michael Bernstein. He had a beautiful vision in creating the Hacienda Home, and Gulf Coast Jewish and Family Services was his life work and passion. He understood the limited resources in Florida for mental health and social services during that time. That's why he founded and grew the organization to respond to underserved populations. Michael was a strong advocate for the downtrodden and for stigmatized populations—the elderly with mental illness and those with HIV. He worked with the HIV population when no one even wanted to talk about it.

Sadly, Bernstein, whose life work involved healing for those with mental and physical illness, took his own life in 2009, six weeks after Caroline's departure from the organization.

"Michael did so much good for so many throughout the years," Caroline attested. "Although there was controversy during his last year with the organization, I feel he deserves to be remembered for his contributions over the decades."

Final Years of the Hacienda Home

Declared a historic landmark in 1996, the aging Hacienda Home qualified for federal block grant funding to replace its roof, overhaul its electrical and plumbing systems and repair its termite damage.

By the turn of the twenty-first century, downtown New Port Richey had experienced a sharp decline. A survey determined the area had become blighted. Businesses fled to U.S. 19 and the local mall. Spaces became vacated or underutilized. Structures were now derelict. The city mobilized and formulated a redevelopment plan.

"The deteriorating building became expensive to maintain," Caroline recalled. "It became cost-prohibited to continue services in the structure."

In 2004, New Port Richey's Community Redevelopment Committee unanimously voted to purchase the Hacienda Home from Gulf Coast Jewish Family Services for $2.2 million. The former owner had two years to vacate the premises, but services continued.

The next year, a developer envisioned transforming the hotel into a special events venue like the Lyceum on Mirror Lake in downtown St. Petersburg and Tampa Theatre, offering concerts and independent films for the city's

The former Hacienda Hotel declined following its closure as a residential treatment facility in the early twenty-first century. *West Pasco Historical Society.*

The Hacienda's courtyard illustrates the property's sharp decline over the preceding two decades. *Photograph by John M. Tevlin, West Pasco Historical Society.*

growing younger population, as reflected by the 2000 census. The city had no such cultural center, and residents had to travel nearly sixty minutes one way to Pinellas or Hillsborough Counties for entertainment. Unfortunately, the developer withdrew in 2006.

The Hacienda remained vacant for almost two decades—nearly a generation.

21

JIM GUNDERSON

The Private Investor Who Saved The Hacienda

On Thursday evenings, after a one-hundred-mile drive from the Lakeside Inn, his historic hotel in Mount Dora, Jim Gunderson checks into his second historic hotel, The Hacienda, for his weekly visit. The hotelier orders a bourbon on the rocks, sits in a white lacquered rocking chair on the veranda overlooking Sims Park and enjoys the sights and sounds of activity as the evening winds down.

Gunderson is a hotelier with respect for history.

In July 2018, Mayor Rob Marlowe and Hacienda Hotel Florida Corporation president Jim Gunderson officially signed the agreement for the historic Hacienda Hotel. "I am pleased that we have taken this next giant step toward The Hacienda reopening as the jewel of downtown New Port Richey," Marlowe said in a news release. "We are thrilled to have the opportunity to be involved with bringing this wonderful and historic hotel back to life," Gunderson said. "I can't wait to get started."

Architects estimated the cost to complete The Hacienda's restoration and renovation would approach $10 to $12 million.

Gunderson, the most qualified of all the prospective hoteliers, had spent forty years as a hospitality industry manager for Marriott Hotels and Naples Beach Hotel and Golf Club. In 2010, he and wife, Alexandra, relocated to Mount Dora in Lake County from Naples after they purchased and extensively restored the Lakeside Inn, Florida's longest continuously operating hotel. Built in 1883, the Lakeside Inn hosted President Calvin Coolidge and his wife, Grace, who visited for a month in the winter of 1930 after the completion of Coolidge's presidency.

Left: Jim Gunderson welcomes The Hacienda's first guests in decades at the hotel's grand opening gala in September 2022. *Photograph by Tim McClain.*

Opposite: The hotel's restoration process invigorates and enthuses residents who have championed its return to its former glory. *West Pasco Historical Society.*

Listed in the National Register of Historic Places, Lakeside Inn and its ninety rooms and suites in five buildings overlook Lake Dora. The complex had faced probable demolition before Gunderson saved it. The Gundersons would accomplish the same for The Hacienda.

Unforeseen when Gunderson signed the agreement, The Hacienda's restoration faced unprecedented challenges, including an international pandemic and supply delays. But he persevered with creative workarounds.

About 80 percent of the hotel was gutted. Much of the structure was stripped down to its exterior brick walls. On the second and third floors, new interior stud wall partitions reconfigured the guest rooms and suites. The iconic arch to the dining room and the hotel's corbels, fireplace and lobby ceiling beams were restored.

Gunderson returned to the hotel's original hotel footprint, eliminating the unsightly additions to the structure that had been built over the decades. He sent out the original wrought iron chandeliers and ornate finials for cleaning and restoration.

While Gunderson had hoped to restore the original wood floor in the hotel lobby, extensive damage required their complete replacement. He repurposed some of the original cypress wood in creating the current front desk and bar.

Although The Hacienda offered a solid façade, rotting wood and quirky attempts at repairs over the decades slowed the restoration process. Extreme changes needed to be made to the bones of the building, and new challenges arose but were tackled as they came up. The addition of an elevator,

absent from the original design in 1927, complied with requirements of the Americans with Disabilities Act.

Some of the hotel's features had to be sacrificed. Two sets of double arches with twisted columns in the hotel's lobby, a signature of architect Thomas Reed Martin, became a solid wall for the relocated and enlarged reception desk and a rectangular opening, providing a grander view of the curved stairway and landing adorned by ornamental wrought iron railings.

Gunderson gathered a team of hospitality professionals with experience in extraordinary service and a reverence for history to carry on the hotel's tradition.

"Being a part of the restoration and reopening of The Hacienda has been one of the highlights of my career," proclaimed Dylan Leigh Gamez, originally from Long Island.

> *When I applied for the marketing and public relations position at Lakeside Inn, I didn't know at the time I'd also be working at The Hacienda. Pink was always my favorite color growing up—thanks to* Power Rangers—*and when I first saw New Port Richey's crown jewel in all her "Calming Coral" glory, it was love at first sight. I've always loved traveling to historic places, and now I get the opportunity to be a part of others' adventures through time every day. Seeing The Hacienda come back to life while still embracing and honoring its history has been a wonderful experience.*

Jim Gunderson (*center*) led the restoration of The Hacienda in 2019. He was supported in this endeavor by the Friends of the Hacienda Hotel and Historic New Port Richey, represented by Gary Gann (*left*) and Bob Langford (*right*). *West Pasco Historical Society*.

Rafe Banks and Danny Banks, spouses in their personal lives, contribute their individual and collective exuberance as hosts of The Hacienda in their professional lives.

"Walking into The Hacienda is like stepping back in time," Rafe Banks, the hotel's general manager, told this author. "The care taken to restore the Pink Lady to her original glory amazes me. It's a beautiful place to work and be a part of. I hope it continues to draw people to New Port Richey so they can experience this historic town to the fullest while staying in the place that first drew so many here nearly a century ago."

"It's been my great pleasure to participate in bringing this historic hotel back to life," remarked Danny Banks, the hotel's food and beverage manager.

So many who remember The Hacienda in its early days have visited after the restoration. They had witnessed its changes over the decades and its closure for a long period. It's an honor and privilege for me to be a part of the revitalization of this iconic Florida landmark. I am thrilled that the hotel is thriving and bringing so many people from all over the world to our little piece of paradise. New Port Richey is a gem and will only continue to prosper as we celebrate its renaissance centennial.

The original arches were visible in the lobby during restoration in 2019. *West Pasco Historical Society.*

The original arches were modified during the hotel's lengthy restoration. *West Pasco Historical Society.*

Oscar Vitacco-Robles, who is now retired from a long career in corporate America, fell in love with The Hacienda during its grand reopening gala and immediately aspired to join its team. At the event, Oscar introduced himself to Rafe Banks and scheduled an interview for the following week. As a front desk concierge, Oscar now boasts the moniker "ambassador of The Hacienda."

"Meeting guests from around the globe is my favorite experience at The Hacienda," Oscar proclaimed. "We've hosted guests from Japan, Canada and Europe. I always provide visitors with the history of our quaint downtown in addition to the hotel and its litany of intriguing, famous guests."

In the hotel's first year of operations, readers of the *Tampa Bay Times* voted The Hacienda as the Best Hotel of 2023. The readers of *Creative Loafing* nominated The Hacienda as Tampa's Best of the Bay for the Best Hotel, Best Place for a Wedding, Best Pasco Restaurant and Best Hotel Bar.

Despite these accolades, Gunderson remains unassuming. As a true historian and realist, he recognizes that buildings often live on after the passings of the individuals who built, purchased, inhabited and restored them. The memories of these individuals fade with the passing of those who remember them, but the bricks and mortar remain for centuries.

"Hopefully, The Hacienda will still be here long after I'm gone."

The Hacienda's Floridian coral hue and Mediterranean Revival architecture contribute to the hotel's identity as a Suncoast social and cultural center. *The Hacienda Hotel.*

The restored courtyard and babbling fountain soothe guests upon arrival. *Photo by Tim McClain.*

In alabaster rocking chairs facing the plaza and Sims Park, guests enjoy coffee or cocktails. *The Hacienda Hotel.*

Lush natural landscaping surround New Port Richey's crown jewel. *The Hacienda Hotel.*

The Hacienda's original east entrance on Bank Street complements the grand courtyard and fountain on the south side of the property. *The Hacienda Hotel.*

The Hacienda's north plaza overlooking Sims Park serves as a tropical venue for weddings and special events. *The Hacienda Hotel.*

Adjacent to the Cotee River and historic Sims Park, the Hacienda Hotel is the heart of downtown New Port Richey. *The Hacienda Hotel.*

Above: Guests are transported back in time to New Port Richey's original heyday when the quaint town became a destination for celebrities and dignitaries. *The Hacienda Hotel.*

Opposite, top: The elegant front desk and hotel bar were carefully constructed using reclaimed wood from the hotel's restoration. *The Hacienda Hotel.*

Opposite, bottom: Guests discover original accents and architecture from the 1920s, all complemented by modern amenities. *The Hacienda Hotel.*

The lobby boasts the hotel's original and painstakingly restored beams, corbels and fireplace. *The Hacienda Hotel.*

Guests can experience what it may have been like to frequent the hotel in the early twentieth century. *The Hacienda Hotel.*

Ornate antiques and original architectural pieces adorn Sasha's on the Park, the hotel's historic dining room that was frequented by luminaries of the twentieth century. *The Hacienda Hotel.*

The Hacienda features forty unique rooms, each styled with classic elegance reminiscent of the hotel's Spanish-Floridian charm. *The Hacienda Hotel.*

The hotel restaurant offers a private dining room, once the original cocktail lounge, for intimate events. *The Hacienda Hotel.*

BIBLIOGRAPHY

Anderson, Dave. "Sarazen's Century of Perspective." *New York Times*, May 16, 1999.

———. "Sports of the Times; Gene Sarazen at 80." *New York Times*, June 18, 1982.

Arizona Daily Star. "Screen Actress Dorothy Dalton Dies at 78." April 16, 1972.

Atchison Daily Globe. "Sensational Finish." March 16, 1908.

Atlanta Georgian. "Actress Returns to America Both to Play and Get Rid of Husband." August 20, 1912.

Atlanta Journal. "The Talk of New York." August 15, 1931.

Avery, Elroy McKendree. *The Genesis of New Port Richey*. New Port Richey, FL: Avery Library and Historical Society, 1924.

Bacon, Deborah. "Alternative for Elderly Ill to Open." *Tampa Tribune*, May 26, 1986.

———. "Hacienda House a Thrifty Alternative to Nursing Care." *Tampa Tribune*, June 17, 1986.

Beckley, Lindsey. "George Ade, Everybody's Friend." *Indiana History Blog*. January 10, 2022. https://blog.history.in.gov/george-ade-everybodys-friend/#:~:text=George%20Ade%2C%20courtesy%20of%20Alchetron,his%20attention%20to%20just%20that.

Benbow, Charles. "Winnifred Long, Grand Dame of Suncoast Art." *St. Petersburg Times*, August 21, 1975.

Berkshire Eagle. "Raymond Hitchcock; His Art All His Own; Visits to Pittsfild Recalled." November 29, 1920.

Boston Globe. "Raymond Hitchcock Dies Suddenly." November 25, 1929.

Bowman, Frank A. "New Port Richey Now Ready for Tourists." *Tampa Tribune*, February 20, 1927.

Brooklyn Daily Eagle. "Raymond Hitchcock Dies of Heart Stroke in Auto at Wife's Side." November 25, 1929.

Brooklyn Daily Times. "Hitchcock's Home a Mass of Ruins." August 31, 1909.

———. "Raymond Hitchcock Dies of Heart Disease in Auto; Falls on Wife's Shoulder." November 25, 1929.

Bruccoli, Matthew J. "A Literary Friendship." *New York Times*, November 7, 1976. https://fitzgerald.narod.ru/bio/bruccoli-ringscott.html.

Buffalo Sunday Morning News. "How Long Do Theatrical Marriages Last?" October 6, 1912.

Caballo, Marion. "Hollywood at Home: Cinema History in Queens, New York City." *Science Survey*, April 27, 2022.

Cannon, Jeff. *New Port Richey: Then & Now*. Charleston, SC: Arcadia Publishing, 2011.

———. "Riding Down Memory Lane on New Port Richey's First Mass Transit System." *Patch*, March 25, 2011. https://patch.com/florida/newportrichey/riding-down-memory-lane-on-new-port-richeys-first-mas6bbe65b308.

Carley, Ruby. "An Aging Beauty Staging Comeback." *St. Petersburg Times*, October 27, 1974.

Carozza, Adam J. "New Port Richey: Myth and History of a City Built on Enchantment." Master's thesis, University of South Florida, 2009. https://digitalcommons.usf.edu/etd/1889.

Chicago Tribune. "Charlotte Greenwood Dies, Stage, Film Comedienne." February 14, 1978.

Citizen-Republican. "Actress Gets Awful Note; $5,000 Demand." December 16, 1909.

Courier. "Can't Find Hitchcock." November 3, 1907.

Cushing Daily Citizen. "Donaldson Is Gone His Songs Still Live." July 20, 1947.

Cutter, John. "Lakeside Inn Marks 10 Years Under New Owner." *Orlando Sentinel*, December 12, 2020.

Dade City Banner. March 3, 1926.

———. March 12, 1926.

———. December 20, 1927.

———. January 27, 1928.

———. October 30, 1936.

Dalrymple, Dolly. "Raymond Hitchcock, with New Vista, Seen as More Colorful Than Ever." *Selma Times-Journal*, January 31, 1926.

Davis, Lisa A. "Langford Retains Seat on Council." *Tampa Tribune*, April 13, 2005.

Dayton Herald. "Search for Comedian Minute." October 31, 1907.

Dayton Sunday News. "Eddie Foy and Seven Children, Keith's—Raymond Hitchcock, Victoria." March 4, 1917.

Democrat and Chronicle. "Raymond Hitchcock Dies; Career Began in Auburn." November 26, 1929.

Dorman, Larry. "Gene Sarazen, 97, Golf Champion, Dies." *New York Times*, May 14, 1999.

Dudley, Bill. "Bob Langford: The Man Who Recorded 'Free Bird.'" Tape Op. https://tapeop.com/interviews/137/bob-langford/.

Dunkirk Evening Observer. "Walter Donaldson, Maker of Songs; Dies in California." July 17, 1947.

Elmira Star-Gazette. "Raymond Hitchcock Faces Divorce Suit." August 19, 1912.

El Reno Daily American. "Hitchcock Acquitted." March 16, 1908.

Evansville Journal. "Raymond Hitchcock Disappears Under Criminal Charges." October 31, 1907.

Evening Independent. January 11, 1930.

Evening Star. "Actor the Victim of False Witness." March 16, 1908.

———. "Girls and Hitchcock." March 13, 1908.

Fernald, Helen. "Hacienda Revival Done in Good Taste." *Tampa Tribune*, November 21, 1974.

Florida Peninsular. November 11, 1871.

Fort Myers News-Press. "'Scarface Al' Capone Dies in Miami Villa from Heart Failure." January 26, 1947.

Fottler, Marsha. "Thomas Reed Martin's 1926 Home Is on the Market." *Sarasota Herald-Tribune*, July 30, 2009. https://www.heraldtribune.com/story/news/2009/08/01/thomas-reed-martins-1926-home-is-on-the-market/28881179007/.

Fresno Morning Republican. "Out of a Harem to Fight for Woman Suffrage in America." February 7, 1914.

Glidewell, Jan. "His Hair Is 'Kinky,' His Suits Don't Fit, and His Fans Love Him." *St. Petersburg Times*, October 2, 1976.

Goldenburg, William Smith. "Watchful Waiting!" *Cincinnati Enquirer*, December 1, 1929.

Golden Valley Chronicle. "Theory Advanced that Hitchcock May Be Hiding Behind 'Make-Up.'" November 7, 1907.

Grand Island Independent. "Singer Tiny Tim Dead at 64." December 2, 1996.

Graves, Brian. "New Book Spotlighted NPR Man's Music Career." *Suncoast News*, January 10, 2020. https://www.suncoastnews.com/news/new-book-spotlighted-npr-man-s-music-career/article_6a0a24d6-324f-11ea-b61a-e3e088583d9a.html.

Great Falls Tribune. "Hitchcock on Stand." June 10, 1908.

Grumet, Bridget Hall. "Fivay: An Aristocratic Boomtown Goes Bust." *Tampa Bay Times*, September 21, 2009.

Haase, Sally. "The Apostles of the Sacred Heart of Jesus of Higganum: And Interview with Sister Doretta D'Albero." HK Now. March 10, 2020. https://hk-now.com/the-apostles-of-the-sacred-heart-of-jesus-of-higganum-an-interview-with-sister-doretta-dalbero/.

Hairston, Hazel. "Flora Hitchcock Stand By." *New York Daily News*, December 8, 1929.

Harper, James. "Frankie Fontaine." *St. Petersburg Times*, October 30, 1976.

Hartford Courant. "Raymond Hitchcocks Have Separated." August 19, 1912.

Hartig, Mikki. "Architect Thomas Reed Martin and Sarasota." *Sarasota Herald-Tribune*, June 18, 2011. https://www.heraldtribune.com/story/news/2011/06/18/architect-thomas-reed-martin-and-sarasota/29023468007/.

Hedman, Carol Jeffares. "History Has Vast Reach in City." *Tampa Tribune*, October 10, 2003.

Henley, J.A. "History of Pasco County, Florida." https://www.fivay.org/hendley.html.

Henry, Mike. "City Will Honor Golfer Sarazen." *Tampa Tribune*, December 30, 1999.

Herald Democrat. "Fear Actor Is Kidnapped." November 1, 1907.

History of Pasco County. "The Hacienda Hotel." https://www.fivay.org/hacienda.html.

International Movie Data Base. https://www.imdb.com/.

Ithaca Journal. "Ed Wynn Dies at Age of 79." June 20, 1966.

Karnowski, Steve. "Tiny Tim Dead of Apparent Cardiac Arrest While Singing 'Tiptoe Thru' the Tulips.'" *Napa Valley Register*, December 2, 1996.

Keefe, Robert. "Council Picks Sarazen Over Swanson." *Tampa Bay Times*, February 3, 1993.

———. "Do These Celebrities Get Tributes? Yes, Lots." *Tampa Bay Times*, January 13, 1993.

Klansne, Nick. "Dinner Theatre Hits Pasco with 'The Fantasticks.'" *Tampa Tribune*, April 23, 1982.

Kooper, Al. "How I Discovered Lynyrd Skynyrd." *Louder*, October 21, 2021. https://www.loudersound.com/features/how-i-discovered-lynyrd-skynyrd-by-al-kooper.

Kornacki, Steve. "Rocker Turned Deputy Mayor." *Tampa Tribune*, July 7, 2005.

———. "'20s Star Power Boosted City's Name." *Tampa Tribune*, July 26, 2003.

Leavenworth Post. "Hitchcock Free Upon One Count." March 16, 1908.

Leavenworth Times. "Motor Admits Motoring with Girl Children." October 29, 1907.

Lincoln Star. June 4, 1933.

Los Angeles Evening Citizen News. "Leon Errol Dies of a Heart Attack at 70." October 12, 1951.

———. "Leon Errol's Former Wife, Dancer, Dies." November 8, 1946.

Los Angeles Evening Express. "Turk Women Vote? Why Not? Wait, See." May 5, 1913.

MacManus, Elizabeth. "In the Early 1900s, Fivay Rose and Fell with Its Sawmills." *Tampa Bay Times*, September 16, 2005.

Macon News. "Very Strange Discovery About Champion Sarazen's Romance." February 10, 1924.

Martin, Susan Taylor. "A Gem Is Restored with Hacienda Hotel in New Port Richey." *Tampa Bay Times*, August 7, 2022. https://www.tampabay.com/life-culture/bay-magazine/2022/08/07/a-gem-is-restored-with-hacienda-hotel-in-new-port-richey/.

———. "Hacienda Rebirth." *Tampa Bay Times*, September 11, 2022.

McIntyre, O.O. "Giving the World the O.O.-McIntyre." *Atlantic City Press*, June 4, 1933.

Meares, Hadley Hall. "Gloria Swanson Was More Than Ready for Her Close-Up." *Vanity Fair*, October 2021. https://www.vanityfair.com/hollywood/2021/10/gloria-swanson-autobiography-sunset-boulevard.

Miami Herald. "Dorothy Dalton, 78, Film Star." April 16, 1972.

———. "George Ade Suffers Nervous Breakdown." February 4, 1932.

Miami News. "Broadway Moves to the Beach." February 18, 1932.

Michaels, Will. "A New Look at Al Capone in St. Pete—Part 1." *Northeast Journal*, July 16, 2015. https://northeastjournal.org/a-new-look-at-al-capone-in-st-pete-part-1/.

Midland Empire News. "Girl Alleges Mistreatment." June 9, 1908.

Miller, Jeff. History of Pasco County, Florida. https://www.fivay.org/index. html.

Miller, Michele. "Bringing New Port Richey's Hacienda Hotel back to Its Old Glory." *What's What New Port Richey*. August 29, 2021. https:// whatswhatnewportrichey.com/bringing-new-port-richeys-hacienda-hotel-back-to-its-old-glory/.

———. "Former Glory of Hacienda Hotel Is in There, Somewhere." *Tampa Bay Times*, September 25, 2019. https://www.tampabay.com/ news/pasco/2019/09/25/former-glory-of-hacienda-hotel-is-in-there-somewhere/.

———. "Returning to Glory." *Tampa Bay Times*, September 27, 2019.

Missoulian. "Girl Forced to Tell Lie to Jury." March 17, 1908.

Montana Record-Herald. "Valet's Story of the Visit." June 10, 1908.

Morning Press. "Raymond Hitchcock—Must Leave Tour." February 12, 1908.

Muir, James. "Three Headed for Broadway." *Dayton Daily News*, August 18, 1931.

Neill, Wilfred. "Famed Comedian Ed Wynn Once Lived and Worked in New Port Richey." *Tampa Bay Times*, January 3, 1979.

———. "Hacienda Built for Movie Stars." *Tampa Bay Times*, October 27, 1974.

Nevada State Journal. "Gene Sarazen Sues for $60,000 Salary." October 20, 1932.

New Port Richey Press. April 11, 1924.

———. November 14, 1924.

———. March 13, 1925.

———. September 4, 1925.

———. October 23, 1925.

———. January 1, 1926.

———. February 5, 1926.

———. February 19, 1926.

———. February 26, 1926.

———. March 5, 1926.

———. March 19, 1926.

———. March 26, 1926.

———. April 16, 1926.

———. June 18, 1926.

———. June 25, 1926.

———. August 13, 1926.

———. August 20, 1926.

———. August 27, 1926.

———. September 10, 1926.

———. November 19, 1926.

———. December 10, 1926.

———. December 17, 1926.

———. January 21, 1927.

———. February 4, 1927.

———. February 18, 1927.

———. April 15, 1927.

———. September 2, 1927.

———. October 21, 1927.

———. November 3, 1927.

———. October 4, 1929.

———. December 20, 1929.

———. January 2, 1930.

———. January 17, 1930.

———. January 24, 1930.

———. January 31, 1930.

———. February 7, 1930.

———. February 14, 1930.

———. March 7, 1930.

———. November 12, 1930.

———. January 6, 1931.

———. January 9, 1931.

———. January 13, 1931.

———. January 23, 1931.

———. February 6, 1931.

———. February 13, 1931.

———. November 3, 1931.

———. February 2, 1934.

———. February 16, 1934.

———. October 5, 1934.

———. November 23, 1934.

———. March 15, 1935.

———. May 10, 1935.

———. October 6, 1939.

———. November 24, 1939.

———. December 15, 1939.

———. December 22, 1939.

———. December 19, 1941.

———. December 22, 1944.

———. August 31, 1945.

———. February 7, 1947.

News-Journal. "The Hearst Libel Suit." November 20, 1907.

News Leader. "Hitchcock Under Arrest." October 29, 1907.

New York Daily News. October 8, 1968.

———. "Flora Zabelle Returns to Stage." September 6, 1931.

New York Times. "Ring Lardner Dies; Noted as Writer." September 26, 1933.

———. "Thomas Meighan, Movie Actor, Dies." July 9, 1936.

New-York Tribune. "R. Hitchcock in a Scene." July 7, 1912.

Niles Daily Star. "Ring Lardner Dies." September 26, 1933.

O'Brien, Lucy. "Relics of the Silent Screen." *Tampa Tribune*, November 6, 1960.

O'Connor, Joanne. "Auburn's Yankee Doodle Dandy." *Citizen*, July 2, 2014.

O'Connor, Tom. "Sapphire and Mink Coat Linked to Hotel Dispute." *Tampa Tribune*, July 7, 1954.

Orlando Sentinel. February 25, 1913.

Oroville Daily Register. "Hitchcock Back to Stand Trial." November 7, 1907.

Overton, James L. "Guy Lombardo Dead at 75." *Herald*, November 7, 1977.

Parsons, Louella O. "Ed Wynn Will Make Picture for Paramount." *Tampa Bay Times*, November 18, 1926.

Patch. "Who Gave Enchantment Park to New Port Richey?" August 4, 2011. https://patch.com/florida/newportrichey/who-gave-enchantment-park-to-new-port-richey.

Perry, Linda. "Fire Code Violations Found in Hotel." *Tampa Bay Times*, May 20, 1982.

Philadelphia Inquirer. "Charlotte Greenwood, 87, Phila.-Born Actress." February 15, 1978.

Pittsburgh Post-Gazette. January 2, 1927.

Rado, Diane. "Hacienda Proposed as 'Special Site.'" *Pasco Times*, n.d.

Railway Age Gazette. August 16, 1912.

Reporter Dispatch. "Dorothy Dalton Silent Star." April 15, 1972.

Rigney, David. "The Historic Places of Pasco County by James J. Horgan, Alice F. Hall and Edward J. Herrmann." *Tampa Bay History* 14, no. 2 (1992): 1–88. https://digitalcommons.usf.edu/tampabayhistory/vol14/iss2/10.

Roberts, Joe. "Guy Lombardo: Old Acquaintance Not Forgotten." *Valley News*, December 28, 1977.

Ross, Sandy. "Bringing Seniors Home from the Hospital." *Tampa Tribune*, September 24, 1991.

San Francisco Call. "Flora Zabelle to Leave Hitchcock." August 18, 1912.

Sarasota History Alive. "Burns Court Historic District, Buildings: Sarasota History." City of Sarasota Public Records. http://www.sarasotahistoryalive. com/index.php?back=history&src=directory&srctype=detail&refno=705 &category=Buildings&view=history&submenu=home.

Shearer, Stephen Michael. *Gloria Swanson: The Ultimate Star.* New York: Thomas Dunne Books, 2013.

Simon, Alexandra. "The Untold Truth of Lynyrd Skynyrd's Billy Powell." Grunge. March 6, 2022. https://www.grunge.com/635562/the-untold-truth-of-lynyrd-skynyrds-billy-powell/.

Sims Family Cemetery. "George Reginald Sims." https://www. simsfamilycemetery.org/George%20Reginald%20Sims/George%20 Reginald%20Sims.html.

Soberances, Bill. "Bill Soberances." *Petaluma Argus-Courier*, April 6, 1983.

Songwriters Hall of Fame. https://www.songhall.org/.

Standard Star. "Gene Sarazen Sues for $40,000 Salary as Pro in Florida." October 20, 1932.

Star-Phoenix. "Answers to Charge." November 6, 1907.

Stevens, Bill. "Hacienda Hotel Offers the Elderly the Life of 'a King.'" *Tampa Bay Times*, May 26, 1977.

St. Petersburg Times. August 9, 1925.

———. February 28, 1962.

———. "Al Capone Pays Visit to the City." February 10, 1931.

———. "Beautification Plans Studied by Men's Club." January 21, 1934.

Suncoast News. "Hacienda Hotel Lease Agreement Becomes Official." July 24, 2018. https://www.suncoastnews.com/business/hacienda-hotel-lease-agreement-becomes-official/article_d63fbd5c-8f83-11e8-bd47-b3d68990b381.html.

Sun-Journal. December 19, 1939.

Swanson, Gloria. *Swanson on Swanson.* New York: Random House, 1980.

Tampa Bay Times. December 31, 1925.

———. "Guy Lombardo Had Interest in Bay Area." November 11, 1977.

Tampa Daily Times. January 20, 1912.

———. February 12, 1912.

———. January 28, 1928.

———. "Coming Soon to Florida." January 1, 1930.

———. "Court Settles Ownership of Richey Hotel." April 9, 1955.

———. "'Hell Harbor' Premiere Set for Jan. 26." January 8, 1930.

———. "Tampa Is Anticipating Second Annual Horse Show Wednesday and Thursday." January 18, 1930.

Tampa Tribune. November 13, 1913.

———. December 29, 1915.

———. January 3, 1926.

———. January 15, 1926.

———. March 24, 1926.

———. November 12, 1926.

———. February 6, 1927.

———. January 8, 1930.

———. January 11, 1930.

———. September 4, 1932.

———. October 23, 1949.

———. January 9, 1954.

———. May 27, 1954.

———. May 30, 1954.

———. February 19, 1957.

———. March 6, 1965.

———. "Boom-Time N. Port Richey Hotel Is Damaged by Fire." June 7, 1968.

———. "Dinner Opens Hotel at New Port Richey." February 18, 1927.

———. "Grey-Little." August 5, 1962.

———. "Hacienda Hotel Receiver Asked in Federal Court." June 5, 1954.

———. "Hacienda Hotel Reported Sold at New Port Richey." March 27, 1959.

———. "'Hell Harbor' to Be Shown Here Jan. 26." January 8, 1930.

———. "Hotel to Reopen." October 1, 1955.

———. "New Hacienda Hotel Greets Vacationists to New Port Richey." February 27, 1927.

———. "New Hotel Opens in Tourist Town." February 6, 1927.

———. "New Port Richey Is Booming These Days, Just as in 1916." March 28, 1968.

———. "News of Record." October 18, 1953.

———. "News of Record." December 9, 1953.

———. "Pasco's Film-Star Past: Did Swanson Live Here." May 12, 2007.

———. "Picture Star Plans to Visit New Pt. Richey." January 1, 1930.

———. "Sarazen Comes from behind to Capture Belleair Meet." March 3, 1930.

———. "Sarazen Wins Miami Golf Tourney Fourth Time in Row." January 6, 1930.

———. "Tampan Give Ovation to 'Hell Harbor' at Triumphal Premiere." January 25, 1930.

Tarpon Springs Leader. May 9, 1913.

This Is Great Neck. Great Neck, NY: League of Women Voters of Great Neck, 1983.

Thomas, Bob. "Ed Wynn, Famed Actor, Comedian Dies of Cancer." *Sheboygan Press*, June 20, 1966.

———. "Entertainers to Pay Tribute to Ed Wynn." *Journal News*, June 22, 1966.

Tiegen, Alex. "Meet Bob Langford, City Council Candidate." Patch. March 17, 2013. https://patch.com/florida/newportrichey/meet-bob-langford-city-council-candidate.

Times Union. "Thomas Meighan Dies at 57; Was Idol of Silent Screen." July 9, 1936.

Turner Classic Movies. https://www.tcm.com/.

Virginian-Pilot. "Girl's Brother Took $1,000 from Comedian." December 24, 1907.

Wade, Christian M. "New Port Richey Mayor Keeps Job by 33 Votes." *Tampa Tribune*, April 12, 2006.

Walrath, Jean. "Ed Wynn Was No Fool, But a Real Actor." *Democrat and Chronicle*, June 26, 1966.

Washington Post. "Hitchcock Gives Bond." November 7, 1907.

Weightman, Kenneth. "Revival: Thomas Reed Martin and the Jazz Age Architecture of New Port Richey, Florida." Master's thesis, University of Tampa, 2022. https://utampa.dspacedirect.org/items/63b5a2c6-d81b-4d40-918a-cd0a5ad76390.

Wudarczyk, Jude. "The Miracle Man: The Story of Allegheny's Thomas Meighan." *Allegheny Society Reporter Dispatch*, no. 60 (Winter 2013): 1–5. https://alleghenycity.org/downloads/060%202013%2001%20Winter%20Reporter%20Dispatch.pdf.

Zabelle, Flora. "I Want to Be Understood." *Green Book Magazine*, January 1913.

ABOUT THE AUTHOR

Photograph by Tamera Weyers-Patrick.

As a licensed mental health counselor with thirty-eight years' experience in the field, Gary Vitacco-Robles holds a master's degree in counselor education from the University of South Florida. Since beginning his career in mental health in 1986, Gary has served as an advocate for survivors of trauma and individuals with psychiatric disorders. Beginning in 1994, Gary has worked with children and families who have survived sexual abuse, physical abuse and neglect and youth with sexual behavior problems. Gary is employed by a healthcare organization in the Tampa Bay area, where he serves as the manager of community-based behavioral health services for adults with severe and persistent mental illness. In 2015, Gary was the recipient of the Florida Council on Mental Health's Provider of the Year Award.

Gary is the author of five respected biographies about Marilyn Monroe and was a uniquely qualified researcher to untangle the web of her death in the two-volume *ICON: What Killed Marilyn Monroe*. His acclaimed, definitive two-volume biography, *ICON: The Life, Times, and Films of Marilyn Monroe*, redefined the actor from a mental health perspective for the twenty-first century. His first book, *Cursum Perficio: Marilyn Monroe's Brentwood Hacienda*, remains a fan favorite.

Gary is the writer, coproducer and commentator of the dramatized, multi-season podcast *Marilyn: Behind the Icon*, adapted from his biographies; it is available at BehindTheIcon.com. He is a media personality and has appeared on Fox News channel. Gary is also the coproducer of the film *Marilyn's Dark Paradise*, written and directed by Remi Gangarossa.

Currently, Gary writes the blog *Tampa Bay Author's Social Diary* and is a town historian for New Port Richey, Florida. He is also the administrator and monitor of the popular Facebook group New Port Richey History and a member of New Port Richey Main Street's Design and Art Committees.

Born in New York to a warm Italian family, Gary has resided in New Port Richey since 1975 and has been happily married to Oscar since 1990.